I'm a Christian
So why am I still...

Published in the UK in 2024 by Living Well Publishing

Copyright © David J Cooper 2024

David J Cooper has asserted their right under the Copyright, Designs and Patents Act, 1988, to be identified as the author of this work.

All rights reserved. No part of this book may be reproduced, stored in a retrieved system or transmitted, in any form or by any means, electronic, mechanical, scanning, photocopying, recording or otherwise, without the prior permission of the author and publisher.

Paperback ISBN: 978-1-7385628-0-0
eBook ISBN: 978-1-7385628-1-7

Cover design and typeset by Spiffing Publishing

I'm a Christian
So why am I still...

THE ART OF INNER DISCIPLING

David J Cooper

Contents

PREFACE 13
    Introduction 15

CHAPTER ONE - Healing and recovery are two
separate things 18
    There is no substitute for growth 19
        Harmony over conflict 21
        For growth think relationship 22
    Self-management through better understanding 23

CHAPTER TWO - The Prodigal Son -
Everything you need to know 26
    The family pattern of dysfunction 27
        Addiction and reverse addiction 29
        The unhealthy relationship 32
        Flipping 33
        The attraction of the dead world 34
        The main function of the Rock bottom 35
        'Parts' and the adult presence 37

CHAPTER THREE - What is the medical model? 42
    The medical model - benefits and limitations 43
        The value of our rock bottom 45
    How does the medical model work? 48
    Changing your view of yourself 49
    Dealing with our success and failure 49
    The healthy alternative 51
    Learning to value your unbelief 51

My prayer of gratitude 53
Developing relationships with your disciples 55
Defining your first 'part' 57
How you recognise your parts behaviour 60
From conflict to harmony 63
No Condemnation 65
What is sin? 67
Jesus's prayer for you and me 71
Understanding the relationship between your mind and your brain 74
Science catching up with the Bible 77

CHAPTER FOUR - Jesus and His Disciples 80
Following the Bible 81

CHAPTER FIVE - Inner and Outer discipling 83
Outer Discipling 85
Inner Discipling 86
The Bible as internal and external guidance 86
The quality of your state determines
the quality of your work 87
The flesh and the spirit 89

CHAPTER SIX - Triggering 92
How does my brain get trained in these ways 92
Radical, immediate and naive 95
The four stages of triggering 96
   The first trigger - Chemical 97
The second trigger - mental 97
   The third trigger - verbal 98
   The Fourth trigger - behavioural 98
The nature of the triggered self 99
Certainty 100

Proportion 100
Reactions and Responses 101
Acceptance and rejection 101
We cannot stop reactions! We all have them. 102
God given resources 103

CHAPTER SEVEN - Producing harmony instead of conflict 106
Inner harmony rather than inner conflict 108
Your parts are trying to help you 109
Covering as a strategy of your parts 110
'I' is a complex statement 112
The upper room 113
The house divided against itself 118
Jesus's relationship with the Disciples 120
From an inconsistent 'self' to a set of consistent 'selves' 121
The Construction and role of our parts..................122
The front room and the back room 124
The three choices of the brain...............................126
Option One - the bin 126
Option Two - the memory 126
Option Three - Take a snapshot 127
It's not the feelings but the proportion! 129
The disciples were traumatised.............................130
The disciples were threatened 131
The disciples were attempting to overcome 131

CHAPTER EIGHT - The practice 134
From blended to unblended language 135
The observer position..138
Confirming the Observing position 140

Back to the Prodigal! 143
Re-triggering your core self 146

CHAPTER NINE - Inner Discipleship -
towards harmony and growth 149
    Christ in you 152
    Developing a better relationship with your parts ... 153
    Why is Judas here? 154
    Why is Levi here? 155
    Exiles 156
    Exiling as covering 158
    Understanding the way your disciples
    protect you 158
        Adams covering 159
        Martha's covering 159
    The disciples recognising and following Jesus. 161

CHAPTER TEN - Recognising your parts 164
    Flocking 166
        The herd mentality 166
    Fighting 167
        Grandiosity 168
        Greed 169
        Ambition 169
    Flighting 169
        Doubt 170
        Fear 171
    Freezing 172
        Shame 173
    Becoming your own primary caregiver 174

CHAPTER ELEVEN - My own journey of
inner discipling 177
　　King Baby 178
　　'My addict' 179
　　Voices of influence 180
　　Inner discipling 180
　　My parts 181
　　Learning about my own parts 183

CHAPTER TWELVE - Discipling your parts 186
　　Working in your 'upper room' 189
　　　　The TV screen of consciousness 190
　　　　Separating your parts from your self 190
　　　　　　Appreciation 193
　　　　　　Education 193
　　　　　　Negotiation 193
　　　　　　Different and Better 195
　　　　　　Brains change with evidence 196
　　　　Know your disciples 197
　　　　Call your disciples 200
　　　　Love your disciples 202
　　　　Work with your Disciples 204
　　　　Angry parts 206
　　　　Shamed parts 207
　　　　Anxious parts 209
　　　　Unbelieving parts 210
　　　　Egotistical parts 211
　　　　Grandiose parts 213
　　　　Frightened parts 214
　　　　What will overcoming look like? 215
　　Conclusion 217

I would that in the Church of God we had many sisters at Jesus' feet, who at last would start up under an inspiration and say "I have thought of something that would bring glory to God which the Church has not heard of before. And this will I put in practice that there may be a fresh gem in my redeemer's crown

Spurgeon 1870

PREFACE

Have you ever sat through a sermon where you have been told that you should be doing something but not been told how to do it? Or that something should be happening in your life when it is not? Then this book is for you. How many times have you heard that you should 'not be conformed to this world but be transformed by the renewing of your mind'? But how many times have you been given clear instructions on how to do it? How many times have you been told to 'take every thought captive'? But how? That you are an overcomer and that you can now have peace beyond all understanding? How many times have you returned home from Church inspired by the word and said, "that's it, I'm never doing 'X' again," or "I'm going to be more 'Y' from now on." Or "I should be less 'Z'. Only to fail that same week and return to Church the following week feeling even more like a failure, even more isolated. Wondering if you are a 'real' Christian.

Preaching is making clear what the Bible tells you to do. Teaching is telling you **how to do** what the Bible tells you to do. As a teacher my aim is for you to be able to do what you should do by telling you exactly how to do it! Step by step, point by point. Until you understand the promises of the Bible because you experience them! I will not do this by giving you my ideas, I will do this by showing you Gods word!

Christians struggling with addiction or dependence issues are not the only ones who will find this book helpful. Anyone struggling with relationship issues, anger, depression, or anxiety will also benefit from this approach. It's true that these issues can be doubly difficult for Christians to deal with. Talking about these things in an environment where you are often surrounded by stories of amazing transformation and success can be hard. Society has removed a lot of the taboos around some of these things these days, but in the modern Church it can still be problematic in an atmosphere of unbounded positivity! Or at least the belief that 'everything should be good now' following your conversion.

Be prepared to be challenged as you read about this approach. Especially the way the world has trained you to think about yourself. You will learn how science is now catching up with the Bible and how improving your relationship with yourself and others can be an effective alternative to medical talk of mental illness and spiritual disease. Go for the 'long game' in your personal development, not the 'quick fix' as you follow Jesus' example and teaching. No matter what your past struggles have been, you can find peace 'that passes all understanding', as you move from a **conflicted** self and develop a **harmonised** self, using the resources God has already given you.

Caveat - The methods used in this book may not be suitable for anyone who has a psychiatric diagnosis or long psychiatric history.

Introduction

My name is Dave. I am a Christian and a recovered person. I was an addict for 15 years and I've been 'recovered' for forty years. This means that I know what it is like to be on both sides of the addiction/recovery fence. Or more accurately I know what it is like *for me* to be on both sides of that fence. Working for many years in rehabs, residential treatment and drop-in centres. I have worked extensively in both the Church and secular groups and environments. Training drug workers and therapists. Writing treatment programs and running private Rehabs. The years I spent working in the field have taught me a lot about what works and what does not work when attempting your recovery.

These experiences have affected me in several ways. They have inspired and encouraged me to share my experience and to help people who are suffering. They have driven me to look more into what happened to me and how to understand myself better. And they have reminded me that I still don't know everything! But the most important thing I have seen, and the most important ambition of this book, is to help you to see just how far we have been shifted away from God's view of mankind. There is one technique of the 'evil one' that is particularly difficult to see, which is when man's wisdom is used to steal and destroy our inheritance. More on this later.

When I look back on my early life one of the main things that strikes me is that there is no information that tells us that we are different from others or what we can expect because of that difference. Whether we are perfectly normal or completely abnormal we only know through our experience. Even when I was healed through an amazing encounter with God, there was no information about what had happened to me. I had to make sense of it by thinking and talking, learning, and comparing.

This is what drives my work with people on their Christian journey. I want them to know why they are the way they are and go through what they go through so they can make sense of their experience and see a clear path forward. I also want them to benefit from the tools I have developed to help them do that. Tools I did not have years ago when I was in the same position.

There are no 'quick fixes' in this book, we will be going for the 'long game'. My commitment is to use whatever happens in a day to help me to grow in maturity, in love and in Christ likeness. I want to inspire you to do the same. In fact, it's the only thing I ask my clients to commit to. Good things happen when we commit to learning from everything, not just the things we like or enjoy. Once we understand that we learn the most from the difficult things, we become unstoppable, and our growth becomes inevitable. In this way this approach takes us on a journey of acceptance and growth rather than offering a 'cure'.

Recovering from my 'addicted' lifestyle led to me working with people as they sought their own recovery. I have been called to work with Churches especially in how to support new Christians who were struggling even though they had 'seen the light'. You will learn about the 'medical model' and how it can get in the way of your growth and development, how it has dominated the way we think about ourselves in western culture. The Church's teaching and approach has not escaped this influence and unhelpful Church messages may be another thing you have to overcome.

There is nothing new under the Sun and so the method we will use will come from Jesus' own teaching and example around the disciples. What may be new to you is the way I will ask you to think about yourself, and how to see what man's wisdom has told you about who and how you are. When it comes to spiritual growth, the way we have been taught to think about ourselves as a human being is often largely unhelpful. After I have explained this in detail, I will then offer you a more Biblical view of the human condition, along with an explanation of how this view will help you to overcome and outgrow your difficulties.

As well as the deeper revelations the Bible offers us the book will also include clear instructions about what to do. This includes practical methods you will use on your spiritual journey. This method will look different to different people because God has made every one of us, in some ways, unique. So, learning how to apply these ideas to yourself is a big part of the learning. There is simply no substitute for growth, and I want you to take responsibility for your own development. You should apply these ideas in a way that makes sense to you. Remember, this is not a psychological approach, and it is certainly not based on the medical model. You will be growing as a person by improving your relationships with everything and everybody, starting with yourself.

CHAPTER ONE

Healing and recovery are two separate things

People often don't make a clear distinction between the part God plays and the part they play in their recovery journey. This is one of the main reasons they often find themselves struggling to make progress. Whether you are looking to recover from a serious dependency or addiction or manage your depression, anger or anxiety, you first need to understand that God does the healing, and you do the recovering! I want you to think about your prayer life now. When you attend Church or when you are praying on your own, do you ask God for something you can do for yourself, or do you ask for something only He can do? Once you make this simple and powerful distinction it will become clear what to ask of yourself and what to ask of God in the future.

For years I saw the same people turning up to the same annual conferences with the same issue, praying for the same thing! We should realise that God is more than able to do what we ask of Him, so if it's not happening, it's not because He hasn't got round to it yet, or because He is not able. There is another reason, and it has to do with you not Him. It's from this perspective that we can make this powerful distinction. Ask yourself now, am I asking God to do something I should be doing myself? When we grow it hurts. Making progress is challenging and there is no substitute for growth! Let me explain.

There is no substitute for growth

> DO NOT DESPISE THESE SMALL BEGINNINGS,
> FOR THE LORD REJOICES TO SEE THE WORK BEGIN,
>
> ZECHARIAH 4:10

I want to ask you an important question. When Jesus left the disciples, he breathed his spirit on them and sent them out (John 20:22). Did you ever ask yourself why he didn't do this on day one? He could have saved himself 3 years of arduous work! 3 years of frustration! 3 years of teaching and coping with 12 people who were not always the sharpest tools in the box (Matthew 17:17). So, I want you to ask yourself, because he is God, why did he take three years over this?

I don't know what you came up with, but I believe the real reason is that there is no substitute for growth and development, and this takes time. Again, look at the way God has designed things. Everything from babies to trees start small and grow. Living things develop and mature. God reminds us to honour this in His word "do not despise the day of small beginnings" (Zec 4:10). Even Jesus grew in wisdom (Luke 2:40 and 52) and developed his stature.

If you look at any of the Miracles that Jesus performed, they always involved things that we could not do for ourselves. But he often told people to do things that they could do for themselves! Remember John 8:11 where he tells the woman "Go now and leave your life of sin". Or John 5:14 where Jesus says to the man "see you are well. Stop sinning or something worse may happen to you".

Apply this idea now to yourself and remember that you need to grow and that this will take time. As you will see, it did not only take time but a certain attitude towards ignorance, worldly ambition, greed and evil. You need to develop the same attitude towards the evil nature in you. You need to create some sort of stability to face your issues! This book uses a Biblical approach to understanding and **managing yourself**. Using a method left to us by Christ himself we learn how to create inner harmony. In making the shift away from the way the world defines us (medical model) to the way the Bible describes us, we can learn to work with the 'evil nature' we all have within us. This is what I am calling 'inner discipling' (a lot more on this later)!

But wait! I hear you say. How can we concentrate on the deeper problems and clever things like 'self-management' when we can't even stop what we are doing?! I understand. This is the first of what is many differences between this book and many others on the subject. You may be surprised, if not amazed, to find that we will not be discussing problems very much. This is because the Bible is clear that behaviour is something that is produced by what happens on the inside. Beliefs, attitudes and thinking produce feelings, and these things produce behaviour, and this produces your brain's reactions through the training these things bring. Changing behaviour without first changing beliefs and attitudes forces us to continually enter a battle with ourselves that we are likely to lose. By adopting this approach, you will avoid developing a conflicted self by starting with the inner workings. These differences will create a harmonised self, which will produce better behaviour naturally.

Your behaviour and the way you react to things is something I want you to notice as changing, not something you demand of yourself from day one. When I run my groups, I tell them that they need never tell us what their problem is! This negates the idea of splitting people into specialist groups. We can all sit together, learn together and grow together.

Harmony over conflict

This approach is all about creating a 'harmonised self' which I believe God is asking us to do in John 17 verse 21. Developing a more Biblical view of the human condition you can avoid perpetuating the 'conflicted self' which is made worse by demanding that you must 'behave differently'. No matter what your problem is, the solution is the same, Jesus and his teaching, his word and his example. Once you have him, you already have everything you need!

You will learn how to manage yourself by developing a better relationship between your brain and your mind, or put another way, your flesh and your spirit. The last thing you want to be doing is trying to grow as a Christian whilst you are still hating yourself. So, try to be patient as you first develop a more Biblical understanding of what it is to be a human being. What the Bible teaches us about that, and how neuroscience is catching up with what Jesus taught and how he lived. Once you have this understanding you will be able to deal with your problems and issues more effectively. The chances are that what you are seeing as your main problem in life will dissolve completely!

You will also learn how I started to use my mistakes to grow as a person. How God showed me a coherent view of my addiction and my recovery which became my Ministry. This book will offer you the tools I use with clients, charities and Churches every day. I will show you how to use them to overcome your own issues, dependencies and addictions. My hope for you is that you learn how you can use your everyday experiences to grow into the person you are designed to be.

For growth think relationship

I view all human issues as **relationship issues**. In this approach you grow by improving the health of all your relationships. So, a simpler way of understanding this approach is to say that the first relationship you need to improve is the relationship with yourself (or selves). Once you have improved and developed a better relationship with yourself you will be in a much better position to improve your relationships with everything and everyone else. You will find some things you have been taught will be turned on their heads in this book! Even some things that might seem obvious to you right now. Here are a few that might get you thinking.

Medical approach says……	Biblical approach says……
I need fixing	You are God's masterpiece
I need to stop (using, drinking, gambling)	You need to grow
You get what you need not what you want	You get what you want not what you need
I need to fight as hard as I can	You need to stop fighting
I need to change (be less like me)	I need to grow (be more like you)

Self-management through better understanding

> THEN GOD SAID, "LET US MAKE MANKIND IN OUR IMAGE, IN OUR LIKENESS, SO THAT THEY MAY RULE OVER THE FISH IN THE SEA AND THE BIRDS IN THE SKY, OVER THE LIVESTOCK AND ALL THE WILD ANIMALS, AND OVER ALL THE CREATURES THAT MOVE ALONG THE GROUND."
>
> GENESIS 1:26

We must go right back to the beginning of the Bible to see how God created us, how we are made to be like him, and how we are the pinnacle of his creation. It should not surprise us as Christians that science is slowly catching up with the Bible. There may be no better example of this than the one this book is based upon. Namely, how we should think about ourselves. The Bible taught us this thousands of years ago, and neuroscience is only in the last few decades 'proving' this view to be true. You may have thought of yourself as 'ill' or having an evil spirit because you sometimes do things you said you wouldn't do. Or because you sometimes have 'voices' in your head with 'bad thoughts'. The Bible promises us that we will struggle with these things and neuroscience has now shown these things to be a normal part of life.

The medical model which I will describe shortly, defines you as one thing, but the Bible always defines you as more complex (Genesis 1:26). This is the way God created you and any view that does not include this more complex idea will at best fall short, at worst it will produce a horrible inner conflict. Your commitment to personal growth and development is most effective when you view yourself as God created you. A complex human being. The Jewish word for God is 'Elohim', which is a Plural word. You may have tried extremely hard to make changes in your life and failed. You may be surprised at how much the way you view and think about yourself caused these failures. The medical model has trained us to think of ourselves in a way that produces conflict and does not take account of the complex nature of the human condition.

So, in this first section I am going to start by examining one of the most famous parables in the Bible. This will help you to see the evidence of how the Bible asks us to view and understand ourselves as human beings. And, by way of contrast, I will also include the way the medical model works, how it differs from the Biblical view, and the consequences we face by using it.

CHAPTER TWO

The Prodigal Son - Everything you need to know

> AND HE SAID, "THERE WAS A MAN WHO HAD TWO SONS.
> LUKE 15:11

I often say at my workshops that everything we need to know about addiction, recovery, growth and family dysfunction is in Luke 15 verses 11 to 32, the story of the prodigal. It still amazes me (although it shouldn't) that neuroscience is only now catching up with some of the ideas that Jesus was telling us about two thousand years ago. I will be drawing ideas from this portion of scripture extensively in this book so it's important to familiarise yourself with it. Here are the important things that we will be learning from this parable.

> THE FAMILY PATTERN OF DYSFUNCTION
> ADDICTION AND REVERSE ADDICTION
> THE ATTRACTION OF THE DEAD WORLD
> THE MAIN FUNCTION OF THE ROCK BOTTOM
> 'PARTS' AND THE ADULT PRESENCE

I'm going to introduce them all now one at a time. Firstly in their Biblical context. After that I will go over them again from a therapeutic angle. This will give you a good grounding when these things come up later as I look at them in more detail and they become part of your practice.

The family pattern of dysfunction

Verse 11 *"there was a man who had two sons"*. The story starts with a family structure which tells us that the main context of the story is 'relationship'. More importantly it describes the structure of the dysfunctional family and the way that addiction and reverse addiction are formed, in this case in the two brothers. The younger one being an example of an addictive pattern whilst the older one is an example of the reverse addiction pattern. Dysfunction in the world creates the two extremes depicted through the two sons' attitudes.

Verse 12 *"The younger one said to his father, 'Father, give me my share of the estate.' So he divided his property between them"*. This verse speaks to me about isolation. Ask yourself this, does it seem like this was an idea the younger son had been discussing with anyone? I would say not? By the second verse Jesus is already describing someone who has one foot in the dead world. He is isolated. I will talk about isolation more later and the way neuroscience is telling us that isolation is even worse than we thought it was. For now, we can just accept that *at best* this was something his friends were wrongly agreeing with. Of course, we can also see the selfish nature which goes along with the isolated thinking. If there is only you in your thoughts, then there is no one else to consider! I suspect that this whole attitude was the result of isolated thinking. Any way he got his wish which also speaks to the patient relationship God has with his children.

Towards the end of the story we hear more about the other son. This helps us to recognise the pattern more clearly from the opposite perspective.

Verse 25. *"Meanwhile, the older son was in the field. When he came near the house, he heard music and dancing. 26 So he called one of the servants and asked him what was going on. 27 'Your brother has come,' he replied, 'and your father has killed the fattened calf because he has him back safe and sound". 28 "The older brother became angry and refused to go in. So his father went out and pleaded with him. 29 But he answered his father, 'Look! All these years I've been slaving for you and never disobeyed your orders. Yet you never gave me even a young goat so I could celebrate with my friends. 30 But when this son of yours who has squandered your property with prostitutes comes home, you kill the fattened calf for him!' 31 "'My son,' the father said, 'you are always with me, and everything I have is yours. 32 But we had to celebrate and be glad, because this brother of yours was dead and is alive again; he was lost and is found.'"*

It is at this point that we meet the other brother. As soon as he finds out what has happened his reaction is anger. Now this was not just a small matter of anger. This was a full-on rebellion! The Father had to come out to him! It was so bad that we never actually heard how this was resolved, or if it ever was. Notice the contrast in attitudes. Whereas the **selfish** escape in the younger brother included demanding his share of the inheritance, the **selfless** escape in the older brother attempts to manipulate things out of the Father. He didn't receive because he didn't ask, (James 4:2) and he just became more resentful over the years.

One of the major ways children react to dysfunction is by thinking that it's all their fault! It's just too threatening to believe that our caregivers are at fault (that comes later), so we not only take the blame, we also take the responsibility. We feel we must do something about it! This sense of responsibility from a young child that doesn't have the experience, knowledge or wisdom to handle the difficulty, often leads to the sort of pattern Jesus is talking about in this Parable. Notice the two sons' attitudes. One wants his inheritance immediately. The other complains later when his work and commitment isn't acknowledged. The older brother is resentful of the younger brother and compares them both constantly whereas we have no evidence that the younger brother ever thinks or considers the older brother.

Addiction and reverse addiction

I want you to understand the pattern here. I call it the pattern of addiction and reverse addiction. If we were to distil the two brothers' attitudes down to a sentence it might look something like this;

Younger Son - Addiction	Older Son - Reverse Addiction
Everything in my life will work out if I get everything I want	Everything in my life will work out if everyone else gets what they want

I can't tell you how many times I have seen this pattern in families I have worked with. It is also present when there are more than two siblings. It is present when there has been addiction in the family history but it's often there even when there has been no addiction present in the family history. Think of these two positions as extreme ends of a spectrum. You may not have suffered with addiction or reverse addiction, but your issues may still be on this spectrum.

"The initial reaction to family dysfunction is always towards the 'reverse' position"

Because the 'medical model' will have you thinking of these ideas as a 'diagnosis' I need to stop at this point and remind you that this is not the model we will be using. Because we will be returning to the Biblical model, I want you to think of these differences as 'potentials' rather than fixed diagnosable states. More like human reactions to traumatic events or dysfunction in the family. The initial reaction to family dysfunction is always towards the 'reverse' position. This is because there is a strong feeling that something is missing, and we feel responsible for solving or providing it. Let me explain further.

The effect of any dysfunction in the family on the children can be broadly understood as placing (or dragging) the child into the adult arena, where they have no experience or ability to help themselves. But they must survive and cannot leave. So, what are the options? As youngsters the idea that this is **the adults' fault** is too threatening (that type of thinking usually comes later), so it follows that it must be our fault! So, we enter a period of trying to make things right. This can involve trying to 'parent the parent' or trying to achieve enough to become acceptable to them. As we accept this heavy responsibility we start to become 'other centred', and this starts a shift towards reverse addiction. If we reject this responsibility, we shift towards addiction. Whichever way we go this can become a terrible burden on a young child, later in life it produces all kinds of stress and depression.

It is often around the age of twelve to fourteen that we begin to look for options of how to escape from this terrible responsibility we have felt up to that point. At this age people are 'individuating' or becoming more like themselves. Both 'solutions' the story represents form radical strategies. We either accept the burden of responsibility (reverse addiction) or we avoid it by escaping into selfishness (addiction). For people like you and me selfishness often is the only answer. Addiction means escaping into a world of one and one only!

The unhealthy relationship

> BUT HE ANSWERED HIS FATHER, 'LOOK, THESE MANY YEARS I HAVE SERVED YOU, AND I NEVER DISOBEYED YOUR COMMAND, YET YOU NEVER GAVE ME A YOUNG GOAT, THAT I MIGHT CELEBRATE WITH MY FRIENDS.
>
> LUKE 15:29

There is, of course, another option to becoming an addict. That of staying in the reverse position and sacrificing yourself to the care of others. This is what I call the 'reverse addict' position and can lead to lifelong frustrations. When I meet my clients or their partners, I find many of them in this position. People in the addict position and the reverse addict position act like magnets of opposite poles, each becoming 'stuck' to the other. How many times have I seen the couple come into therapy in these extreme positions? Of course, when they first meet it's like a match made in heaven, because they both want the same thing, they both want the addict to come first! So, at the start they are both getting what they want, but once the 'honeymoon' period wears off it often leads to a chaotic lifestyle.

But wait! I hear you say. Selfless sacrifice to the care of others? Isn't that a good thing? Isn't that what we are supposed to be doing as Christians? Why is that a bad thing? I understand the question. Doesn't it look good. All that giving and putting their partner first. How good did the older brother look in Jesus' parable until the end of the story. It is only when the 'addict' brother begins his recovery journey that the resentment of the older brother is exposed. Only then are all his 'good works' exposed as selfish and manipulative. The Father has to go out to him in the field as he will not even come in to celebrate.

We must remember that there is a world of difference between the older brother's behaviour and the mature decision to offer our lives in sacrifice. People in the reverse addict position might look good but they are just as extreme, needing just as much help and are just as afflicted as their addicted partner, even though they present very differently.

Flipping

It is often only when someone recovers from an addicted or dependent lifestyle that they are reacquainted with their reverse addict past, this 'thing' they thought they had cleverly avoided when they escaped into selfishness. The overwhelming burden of responsibility for others, learned in the past, returns, flipping them into old feelings and thoughts. They will often feel that their only escape is retreating back into their addict lifestyle. I have met many people caught in this unhealthy oscillation between addiction and reverse addiction.

If someone has become dependent rather than addicted, 'flipping' is not always present. Their dependence could have developed more from a sense of protection against some form of mental or emotional issue. But when they try to stop, as the protective layer of drugs or alcohol is removed, what it covered all those years ago is once more revealed.

Understanding this puts you in a much better place to manage the excesses of reverse addiction. As well as major forms of flipping which happen as a result of recovery, there is another form I often notice. This form of flipping can happen daily and depends on the person they are relating to at the time, or the situation they are in. It is from this more 'relational' position that we can understand these things as 'potentials' rather than 'diagnoses.

The 'relational' view also helps you to avoid the medical idea of some sort of illness, affliction, or condition. You can then begin to see the potential in this recovery method. As you can see, the Biblical approach does not start from the classic medical position "what's wrong with you"? Rather it opens the radical possibility that we will be looking at later, that these things are happening because things are working well! Not because they are broken. But for now, back to the story.

The attraction of the dead world

Verse 13 *"Not long after that, the younger son got together all he had, set off for a distant country and there squandered his wealth in wild living"*. It's easy to miss the importance of the word 'distant' here. This is another clue that we are talking about the dead world. It is being described as far away from the world of the Father. Notice in the son's decision he is also choosing **things over people**. Later in this book you will read about the nature of 'triggering' and 'parts'. I believe that the younger son is in a triggered state when he makes these mistakes. You will learn that our younger parts' decisions are **always about now, always naive, and always radical**. Let's look at his thinking in this light. He is taking his whole inheritance, (not to mention how much his family has worked to provide it) and using it to feel better **now**. It's not looking towards the future, so it's **naive,** and it's going against his cultural heritage, so it's **radical**. And, as far as the future goes, it's a disaster.

The main function of the Rock bottom

Verse 14 and 15 *"After he had spent everything, there was a severe famine in that whole country, and he began to be in need. 15 So he went and hired himself out to a citizen of that country, who sent him to his fields to feed pigs. 16 He longed to fill his stomach with the pods that the pigs were eating, but no one gave him anything".* The naivety of his thinking and decision making is now brought home by 'tribulation'. He is now penniless and in trouble and it is here that the nature of 'appearances' is illuminated. He would have had lots of 'hangers on' when he was throwing his money about like water, but they were all gone now. This is not something I would blame them for but notice that the son had been more comfortable with these false relationships than with real ones.

The other thing to notice here is the attitude of the Father. He is not searching out his Son, not trying to bail him out or rescue him. He is waiting patiently at home.

Verse 17,18,19,20 *"When he came to his senses, he said, 'How many of my father's hired servants have food to spare, and here I am starving to death! 18 I will set out and go back to my father and say to him: Father, I have sinned against heaven and against you. 19 I am no longer worthy to be called your son; make me like one of your hired servants.'*

> "WHEN HE CAME TO HIS SENSES, HE SAID,
> HOW MANY OF MY FATHER'S HIRED SERVANTS HAVE FOOD TO SPARE,
> AND HERE I AM STARVING TO DEATH!
> LUKE 15:17

It is common for these 'rock bottom' experiences to be brought about by almost nothing. People expect them to be dramatic affairs where something tragic finally convinces us to change our attitude and direction, but this is rarely the case. Big events tend to harden a person's resolve and make them more set in their ways. The old saying that it is the last straw that breaks the Camels back really applies here.

Take the Prodigal. There was nothing dramatic about his moment with the pigs. It was probably a normal sort of day on the farm. Very much like the day before. But something was about to change forever. In Luke 15:17 he 'came to his senses'. This is a moment that took many years to create and cannot be recreated easily. It was created at a tremendous cost and so I want you to think of your rock bottom as extremely valuable and important to your recovery. Not something to be avoided or 'saved from'.

'Parts' and the adult presence

In this book we will be using the Biblical idea that we are 'multifaceted' and have both the spirit and the flesh living within us. This will be covered in more detail later. For now, let's look at verse 17 of Luke 15 to understand the idea of 'parts' and how Jesus refers to this way of understanding ourselves. Modern versions of the Bible say things like "when he came to his senses", but the ESV says "But when he came to himself" as a description of his 'rock bottom'. I love the Wycliffe version which says, "And he turned again to himself, and said, "how many hired men in my father's house have plenty of loaves; and I perish here through hunger". Just ask yourself now, who is talking to who here? Which self is turning to which self? This is a clear description of the way that human beings are complex and multifaceted, straight from the mouth of Jesus himself. As you will learn later in this book the adult or most grown-up part of the prodigal is turning to the flesh or 'child part' that got him in this position in the first place. When you look at what the 'core' self says, does it seem to you that he was surprised at what was going on? It's as if this part of him had been asleep until now.

Verse 17 has the classic description of a 'rock bottom'. More than the pain and problems which cannot be quantified, rock bottoms are more about coming to your 'self' (your senses) and seeing things in proportion. Rock bottoms are more about seeing reality than they are about the size of the troubles. Notice how the son's appraisal of his situation is now crystal clear. Compare this with his earlier attitude? It sounds like two different people! There is a very good reason for this, and you will hear a lot more about it later. Notice that the only thing that wakes up this 'adult self' is pain and suffering. Only when he got to the end of his ideas and resources did this part of him become activated. Notice also that the strategy of his adult self is to take the more difficult and challenging path. His 'child part' just wanted what he wanted when he wanted it. Comfort and grandiosity, pleasure and lording it over people. His more adult self is willing to face the music.

Verse 20,21,22,23,24 *"So he got up and went to his father. "But while he was still a long way off, his father saw him and was filled with compassion for him; he ran to his son, threw his arms around him and kissed him. 21 "The son said to him, 'Father, I have sinned against heaven and against you. I am no longer worthy to be called your son.' 22 "But the father said to his servants, 'Quick! Bring the best robe and put it on him. Put a ring on his finger and sandals on his feet. 23 Bring the fattened calf and kill it. Let's have a feast and celebrate. 24 For this son of mine was dead and is alive again; he was lost and is found.' So, they began to celebrate".*

In these verses we see the fruit of the rock bottom. At this point his relationship with his father is at its best. Now he has the humility to admit his sin and is prepared to receive his punishment. Until we are ready to face the consequences of our addicted lifestyle, we cannot expect to develop a full recovery.

I want to draw your attention to another clear idea here. Look at everything the younger son does from verse 11 to verse 17 (his rock bottom). Now look at everything he does following his rock bottom. Every decision he makes prior to the rock bottom is disastrous, while every decision he makes after his rock bottom is perfect. Does this not sound like the rock bottom is something unbelievably valuable? And yet families spend years trying to help their loved ones avoid it! More of the value of such moments later.

So, what about the older son? Reverse addicts are filled with an overburdening sense of responsibility for others, a desperate desire to please others, along with a rather fragile sense of their own being as existing only within the value others place on them. Once you see the older brother this way the idea of altruistic motives disappears, and we see someone held captive by a set of errant beliefs. Of course, this leads to massive resentment, and we see the result of this once the father's love for the younger son is revealed. The older brother was apparently fine with the idea of disapproval of the younger son because this was based upon his behaviour. But once the behaviour is not the thing in focus but the relationship, this is when the problems start because the older brother wants to be seen through his behaviour and says as such to the father. *29 But he answered his father, 'Look! All these years I've been slaving for you and never disobeyed your orders. Yet you never gave me even a young goat so I could celebrate with my friends. 30 But when this son of yours who has squandered your property with prostitutes comes home, you kill the fattened calf for him!'*

The Father then corrects the older son by renewing the perspective and placing it back firmly in the idea of the living and dead worlds. At the same time revealing the error of the older son and his whole perspective on life.

31 "'My son,' the father said, 'you are always with me, and everything I have is yours. 32 But we had to celebrate and be glad, because this brother of yours was dead and is alive again; he was lost and is found.'" Here we see a direct reference to the dead world and how we can return from it.

So, this story reveals a pattern I have seen many times in my work with families. Whenever we see dysfunction in a family (which the Bible teaches us is every family) the children must find a way to survive it. In this parable we see the two main ways that children tend to survive these difficulties in the two brothers' attitudes. In the younger brother we see the attitude that can be described as "everything will work out if I get everything I want". This is the 'addict' or selfish escape. In his older brother we see the attitude that can be described as "everything will work out if everybody else gets what they want ". This is the 'reverse addict' or selfless escape. Both are survival strategies and are typical of a family structure I have seen repeatedly in my work. I will say more about both these attitudes later but for now I want to acknowledge yet another example of the latest scientific findings showing us what God's word taught us thousands of years previously. Addiction is the extreme version of a pattern that affects us all.

What happens in the typical addiction scenario? Somebody finally accepts after years of getting worse that they need to do something. That something is usually 'stop'. Drugs or alcohol particularly but other obsessive behaviours and mental issues can result in the same conclusion. The reasoning is understandable, alcohol is the problem, therefore I need to stop, and everything will work out. My anger is the problem, so I need to stop being angry. But we must remember that alcohol did not start out as problem number two, it started out as the solution to problem number one. It only became the main problem later as the consequences of choosing an unhealthy strategy emerged, which they always do. How many times have I heard a new client say to me "I have to stop"!

Of course, our ultimate aim, our future vision for anyone in this position would be for them to be 'clean' but to make it our main aim is a huge mistake. Like making 'happiness' our life goal. So, abstinence should be the **result** of recovery not the **basis** of recovery. I believe that making abstinence our aim sets us up for what I call the trap of success and failure. More of that later. Next, we need to understand why we are not naturally finding these ideas. It's because we have been saturated, soaked in what we might call the medical model.

CHAPTER THREE

What is the medical model?

> "THAT ALL THE INSANE BE TURNED OVER TO THE PHILOSOPHERS
> AND THAT THE MEDICAL MEN STOP MIXING INTO THE
> BUSINESS OF THE HUMAN MIND"
> (KANT I. ANTHROPOLOGY FROM A PRAGMATIC POINT OF VIEW. [TRANSLATED BY MJ GREGOR.]
> THE HAGUE: MARTINUS NIJHOFF, 1974: 82-83.)

Having given you a Biblical view into the human condition and the issues we face, I now want to remind you just how much the medical model differs from the Biblical view. How influential it may have been in your life. Especially in the way you might have approached your personal development and growth.

For at least the last 150 years our western culture has been soaked, you could say saturated, in what I will call the 'medical model'. This powerful way of looking at things arose from the scientific approach. It affects everything we do, especially the way we think about **ourselves**. This is because this way of thinking has been largely accepted as **the** way to think about ourselves. You may be shocked to find how much this view has influenced the way you have managed and related to yourself, not to mention the way it may have influenced the Church you have attended.

It is incredibly influential, especially around our mental and emotional well-being. Thousands of books offer tempting strap lines about how you can 'be a better you'. 'Stop being a failure'. 'Say goodbye to depression' etc. etc. What do most of these books have in common? They are mostly based on the medical model. Most problematic is that, like some other worldly things, it has got into the church. As a result, it has become mixed in with God's teaching and produced as much confusion among the suffering saved as it has the unsaved.

The medical model - benefits and limitations

At the time of writing the world is dealing with a Global pandemic around the Coronavirus. We see photos of this virus on news feeds, and it is a perfect example of how useful the medical model can be. As a 'pathologizing' model it always starts with the same question, "what's wrong with you"? It helps us find cures and vaccines for things like the Coronavirus. This view makes sense because a virus can be seen under a microscope. But let me ask you, can you see an attitude, a belief or even a feeling under a microscope? Of course not.

> THERE IS NO HEALTH IN US
> ANGLICAN PRAYER BOOK (MORNING PRAYER)

So, we can start to see some limits to the medical model. The problem is that our society has become so saturated with this type of thinking that we are now applying it to everything! How many times do you hear yourself and others say, "what's wrong with me"? And "There's something wrong with you". Psychology, based on the medical model, tries to discover 'the problem'. Then to quantify, describe, name, diagnose and cure it. The act of looking for and differentiating between patients' issues leads to an ever-growing number of 'conditions'. The DSM 5 now includes enough diagnosable and nameable conditions that in 2014 more than 50% of Americans were included as suffering from one or another of the growing list of conditions.

Most people would agree that the two main institutions in modern society are the Church and science. When we think of what they have said about the 'parts' of our personality we end up in the same place. One 'demonises' them and the other 'pathologises' them! Either way the two most influential bodies in our world have suggested that these 'parts' need to be fought with and got rid of. Either because they are evil spirits or mental conditions. Neuroscience has blown these ideas out of the water as modern digital research catches up with the Bible!

In Luke 8:43 we read about a woman who was suffering with a bleeding issue that had been untreatable for twelve years. Of course, this was not a 'prodigal son' type of rock bottom as such but let me ask you this. Would she have produced the faith that healed her if she had not suffered for all that time? Faith that drew power from the Lord so much that he asked, "who touched me"? Faith that produced an effect that happened to no one else on that day? Even though many people touched him. Suffering brings moments that cannot be recreated.

The value of our rock bottom

So, what am I saying here? It is based upon an experience of meeting the late great Max Glatt (1912-2002) who authored the book 'alcoholism' which was the text of medical students in Britain for many years and included a diagram something like the one here.

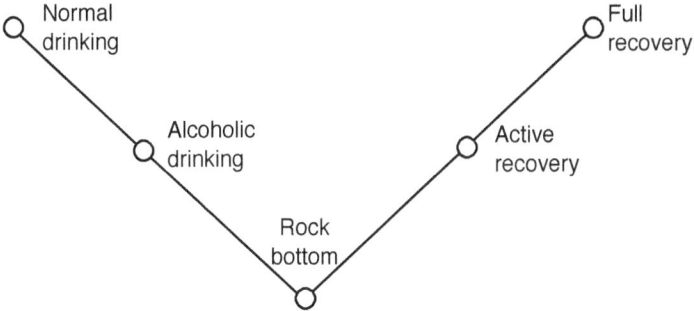

As you can see from my simplified version this diagram has a pronounced 'V' shape. It shows the descent from **normal drinking** all the way down to a **rock bottom** and then maps the journey back up again to a **full recovery**. This is the epitome of the medical model, including as it does the idea that recovery is achieved when we return to the same state as before. But anyone who has overcome these difficulties will tell you that their recovery is far more than that! What would the prodigal say about his recovery?

Even back then in 1988 I always felt that there was something I didn't like about this diagram, even though I had had no training yet and didn't know what it was that I didn't like about it. It was only years later after my training and some professional development of my own that I realised what it was about this 'medical model' that bothered me.

If we take the medical definition of recovery it is defined as being restored to a similar state of health to that enjoyed prior to the condition or illness. You can see this in the diagram where the 'full recovery' is the same height as the 'normal drinking'. But if you ask people that have recovered from addiction, they almost always say that they have become far more than they were previously, and I am one of them! So, we need to acknowledge that recovery from addiction goes beyond the medical concept of an illness. Something more is going on here.

When I run my workshops, I show this diagram and ask what produces the 'full recovery' in our diagram. The 'active recovery' is the answer. And what produces that, I ask. They answer, "The rock bottom". It's at this point that they often begin to see the idea. What produces the rock bottom? The alcoholic drinking! As painful as these observations are to people who care for addicted people (see the section on reverse addicts for more on this). We need to acknowledge that we can spend a lot of time and money preventing the very thing that needs to happen.

So, I wanted to 'straighten out' this 'V' so that the 'bad' bits as well as the 'good' bits are seen as **components of growth**. When we do this, we construct an escape from the constraints and the negative consequences of 'success and failure'. The question "what if all my experiences are leading me to recovery"? What if they are all aspects of recovery? When you fully digest these ideas, you are better equipped to work with yourself in a way that supports your development and your recovery as harmonious achievements rather than battles won.

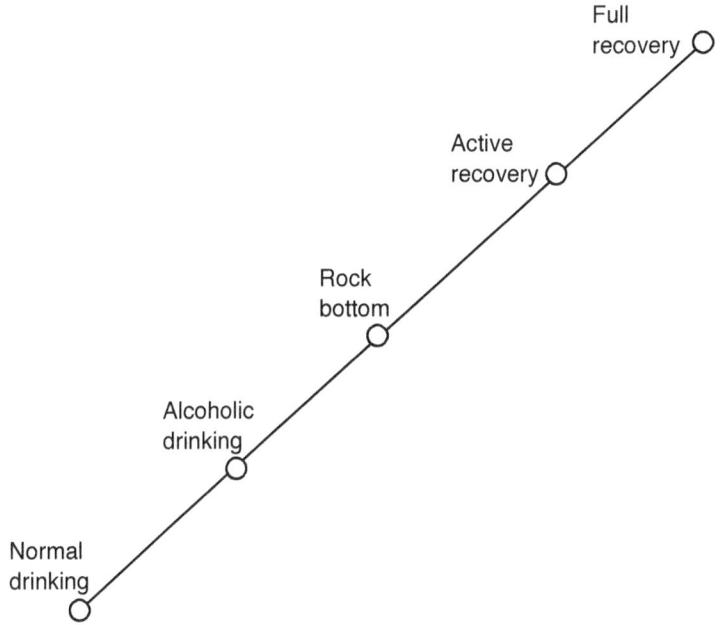

Yes, I know, this is 'hard teaching'. It may take you some time before fully digesting this idea. Essentially it means accepting that you often only get to the good bit through the bad bit. We all want to diminish suffering if we can. When I work with a family, I often support them over this hurdle. I assure them that I am not asking them to stop loving their child, brother, or partner. I am asking them to love them more.

Let's go back to the Prodigal for our learning. Did you notice the father's behaviour in the early part of the story? Would you call this uncaring? He did not stop the son from wasting all his money. He did not chase him or even stay in contact. He waited and watched until the process brought his son back to him.

In Matthew 16:23 Peter is rebuked by the Lord for trying to prevent His suffering. It seems obvious to Peter that the Lord must be protected and is willing to take on the role. Jesus makes him understand that these things must happen for the glory to be revealed. He must get to the good bit through the bad bit. How many times have we delayed the recovery of someone by being overly helpful? Did this delay do any good or is it just a way to make us feel a little better because we are being 'helpful'? If you are in the position of watching someone trying to recover, it's important that you don't delay things by being over helpful. Jesus shows Peter that his thinking is not deep enough. Do we have in mind the things of God or just the things of man?

How does the medical model work?

By starting with the idea of 'what's wrong with you', this model essentially says, "You need to change" or in other words you need to be **'less like you'**. When we are talking about mental or emotional issues, this is like telling a cheetah that it should have stripes rather than spots! Often placing the 'patient' in an impossible position because of the way it creates inner conflict or self-loathing. It often leaves people with a sense that they must change, whilst at the same time defining a self-image that feels inadequate to the task!

Changing your view of yourself

The Biblical approach says just the opposite of the medical model. I am going to show you that becoming **'more like you'** is a much more effective approach when attempting to outgrow your addiction and dependence. You will also learn how Jesus has modelled this for us and offers a God given method.

Of course, the reason the medical model has been so successful in defining the way we think about ourselves is that it matches how we often feel. You know you do things wrong and that you fail and have problems. The medical model echoes your experience by saying that there's something wrong with you and offers ways to 'fix' yourself. This model and the approach it takes has produced a 'self-help' industry that is set to be annually turning over 13.2 billion dollars in 2022. Not to mention a medicinal pill industry which is set to be turning over 1,033 billion dollars annually in 2022. But ask yourself, if these approaches were effective wouldn't they be levelling out or shrinking by now?

Dealing with our success and failure

> I CARE VERY LITTLE IF I AM JUDGED BY YOU OR BY ANY HUMAN COURT; INDEED, I DO NOT EVEN JUDGE MYSELF.
> 1 CORINTHIANS 4:3

Do you think of yourself as a success? Or do you think of yourself as a failure? Do you judge yourself? If you have an aim or a goal, you will have a sense of how well you are doing, so it makes sense to have a useful goal. The most useful goal is your own growth and development as a person. That way you will stay out of the trap of success and failure. No one put it better than the poet Rudyard Kipling in his poem 'if'.

> IF YOU CAN MEET WITH TRIUMPH AND DISASTER AND TREAT THOSE TWO IMPOSTORS JUST THE SAME;

Triumph and disaster are 'success and failure', and he calls them both imposters! He suggests that we treat them both the same, by which he means that we should reject them both. If you think about the product of these states, you will probably agree that success can lead to pride while failure leads to shame! That's where they lead! The last thing you need is to get caught up in these as you cannot think clearly about your situation and how to help yourself from these 'states'. Being an overcomer (1 John 5:5) is a much better aim.

I hope that you can now see the trap of success and failure and maybe you know that you have been caught in it. Please try your best to avoid feeling bad about this, rather concentrate on what you have learned today! (Did you notice what I did there? I got you out of the trap!) I help people to see the trap for what it is and how counterproductive it is. Similarly, you can overcome this trap for yourself. The way you get caught in the trap is through the aim you set and your efforts to 'succeed'.

The healthy alternative

Remember at the beginning of this I called success and failure a 'duality of concepts'. We have just spent some time looking at how these opposites can create a trap which you can become stuck in for years. But what is the alternative? I help my clients aim for something that is not part of a duality but is more of a unity or single thing. Growth!

I tell them that….

> GROWTH PRODUCES ABSTINENCE BUT
> ABSTINENCE DOES NOT PRODUCE GROWTH!

You can think of this simply as a commitment to learning from everything that happens. And when I say everything, that includes your 'rock bottom'. If you have had one.

Remember that I asked you to be prepared to be challenged? A lot of what you will learn here will go against your 'common sense'. Most of all be prepared to follow what God is saying through his design, through his son, and through his word. As we move away from the medical model, I am going to introduce you to a better way of looking at things. It's in the very heart of Jesus' ministry.

Learning to value your unbelief

> THE FATHER INSTANTLY CRIED OUT,
> "I DO BELIEVE; HELP ME OVERCOME MY UNBELIEF!"
>
> MARK 9:24

One of the best examples of this 'different thinking' is one that I see and work with often. If a client is struggling with this idea of the multifaceted self, I explain that if the imagination did not work this way, if it could not work autonomously, we would not have any poetry or architecture, mathematics or science. I sometimes ask the client "when did you become a Christian"? They might say "when I was 20". So, I remind them that any part of them that is less than twenty years of age is not a Christian! So that often helps them to understand that if they started taking drugs at fifteen and only became a Christian at twenty-one, then there is no point calling on the 'drug taking' part to be a 'better Christian', since that part of you is not a Christian!

There is a notable example of this in the Bible when a boy is brought to Jesus by his Father because the disciples could not drive out a demon in the boy. Jesus asks the man to believe and the man answers, "Lord I do believe, help me overcome my unbelief" Mark 9:24 NIV. Here we see belief and unbelief living together in one person, just as they do in me and in you. And here we come to another reason not to hate your parts. I want you to know that, just like the man in Mark 9, all your development from now till the day you die will come from this 'unbelief'. Yes, it will come from your parts. Just like the disciples you will see the transformation of yourself in recovery by winning their trust and encouraging them to become what they were intended to be.

My prayer of gratitude

> PETER SAW HIS OPPORTUNITY AND ADDRESSED THE CROWD. "PEOPLE OF ISRAEL," HE SAID, "WHAT IS SO SURPRISING ABOUT THIS? AND WHY STARE AT US AS THOUGH WE HAD MADE THIS MAN WALK BY OUR OWN POWER OR GODLINESS?
>
> ACTS 3:12

Have you ever thought about the change in the disciples after Pentecost? Have you meditated on the clarity, the calmness and the courage they displayed once they trusted the Lord completely? Have you read in Acts how they spoke out and taught with such boldness and clarity, such as in Acts 4:8 and Acts 7:2. As well as Paul, after his encounter with the Lord later in Acts 13:16. These are amazing transformations by anyone's estimation, but once we understand the process and the fact that it can be duplicated within us, then we can read these exploits with a new understanding and a new enthusiasm. These qualities have now been identified through digital research into the brain's activity. As I said earlier, it should not surprise us that science is eventually catching up with the Bible.

The qualities that research has found to be consistently available as a resource for everyone are

> CALM - CLEAR - CREATIVE - CURIOUS - COURAGEOUS - CONFIDENT - CONNECTED - COMPASSIONATE

Does this remind you of the disciples once they trusted the Lord completely? These are your resources. God breathed his spirit into Adam in the garden and we are all descendants of his. This means that you have within you, resources that come directly from God. Pure, untainted by circumstance, unchanging over time, but not always accessed in experience.

I hope that the difference between this approach and other more traditional 'medical' based approaches is now becoming clearer. It's not about 'changing' and being less like yourself. It's more about making progress by accessing the things God has already given you. Then understanding more about why you have not always been able to access them. I often use this understanding and gratitude for these resources in my prayers. This one I offer here would be typical of how I integrate these ideas into my spiritual life.

Lord, I thank you for the calmness that passes all understanding
Where there was no way, you made a way for me
You gave me courage and confidence
Helping me to think clearly as I face my troubles
Lead me to share your compassion as I connect more with others
Thank you for helping me be creative as I marvel at your creation
Let me never lose the wonder as I meditate on your word.

Notice that I am giving thanks for the qualities mentioned above. Pure calm, courage and confidence. Clarity, compassion and creativity, as well as curiosity and connectedness. Giving thanks for these things, being grateful for what God has already done for us is one way of improving our state and preparing for the challenges ahead.

Developing relationships with your disciples

> THE MIND GOVERNED BY THE FLESH IS HOSTILE TO GOD;
> IT DOES NOT SUBMIT TO GOD'S LAW, NOR CAN IT DO SO.
>
> ROMANS 8:7

Modern research (IFS) is catching up with the Bible and is showing us that we all have this 'adult' or 'core self' inside us. The research has shown that these adult resources are consistent across all colours and creeds, gender and even age. As Christians we know that God breathed his spirit on the dust when he created Adam (Genesis 2:7). The spirit of God is living in everyone. It is this spirit that stands above circumstance and all the things that life throws at you. Whereas your parts are constructed through circumstances. Jesus, who came from heaven, and worked in the spirit, approached the disciples who were oppressed by life.

The idea of the multifaceted self or 'parts' is not new. Freud said that they were demons and should be removed or ignored. Carl Jung first started talking about the way we have parts over one hundred years ago. He called them 'complexes' and worked quite intensively with them for a few years. Psychosynthesis is a therapeutic approach developed by Roberto Assagioli who said in 1910 that

Freud's view of the human being was limited. In other words, it did not include the complexity of the multifaceted self.

After working with hundreds of patients Dr Richard Schwartz found that everyone (not just Christians) had this 'real or true' self within them, and even more amazing, that we can access it without adding anything to ourselves. Rather than learning or receiving anything from anyone, it's much more about rebalancing our parts until they are back to doing what they should and acknowledging the leader (which is the 'grown up'). Through many years of research, he discovered what he calls the 'eight C's of self'. When listening to these as a Christian it was obvious to me that these were descriptions of our Christ likeness.

- Calm
- Clear
- Curious
- Creative
- Confident
- Courageous
- Compassionate
- Connected

I love this especially because the research was not done from a Christian perspective, but doesn't it sound like Jesus! You also need to learn that your parts act in a way that opposes your adult. Just as Paul wrote in his letter (Romans 8:7). When you are 'triggered' your brain takes over and your feeling, thinking, talking and behaviour shift from a spiritual perspective which puts God first, to a worldly perspective that puts you first. As the table below shows.

Calm	Becomes	Crazy
Clear	Becomes	Confused
Curious	Becomes	Certain
Creative	Becomes	Concrete
Confident	Becomes	(un)Confident
Courageous	Becomes	Cowardly
Compassionate	Becomes	Cold
Connected	Becomes	(dis)Connected

These are the feelings or states to look for in yourself that tell you that something has triggered you by appearing to be a threat. When your brain perceives a threat, expect the thoughts and suggestions that go with this to be from the 'parts' perspective. Try this short exercise now to familiarise yourself with this approach.

Defining your first 'part'

Take a sheet of paper and write down the eight 'Cs' on the left, just as it's done above. Now think about a time when you did not feel this way! On the right of the page, opposite the words in the eight Cs column, write the word that best describes the new feeling. It might be different from the list above, or some of the words might be the same. Write down whatever makes sense to you and best describes how you feel when this 'triggering' happens. You might not feel 'crazy' when you lose your calmness, it might be more like 'panic', for instance. Once you have your two columns, say "I am" then read the eight Cs. Then say "but there is a part of me that is" followed by the column on the right.

There, your first unblending exercise! How did it feel? Notice how well you just described this part. Allow yourself to become curious about how old the part is, why it feels this way, and what it might be protecting you from.

In therapy, I use three ideas that describe the typical motivation of your 'parts'. As you get to know your 'selves' better, you will see typical ways that your brain behaves. Parts strategies tend to be

1. Activated by threat - The parts react when they believe you to be threatened so looking for what might be the source of the threat can be a useful way forward.
2. Immediate - there is no timeline in the brain. It's all about now, even if the consequences in the future will be disastrous.
3. Radical - They tend to go for extreme suggestions, but not always. Look out for emergency type suggestions.
4. Naive – Your parts are younger than you and do not have your wisdom or experience. They will always offer solutions and strategies that are naive.

The following is a general list of the type of changes you will experience during these triggered moments.

- Crazy (not caring about the consequences)
- Confused (not knowing what to do)
- Certain (having an agenda)
- Concrete (Seeing only one-way forwards)
- (un)Confident (not believing anything will work out)
- Cowardly (wanting to avoid difficulty)
- Cold (not caring about others)
- (dis)Connected (Having no feeling for others suffering)

Think now about the disciples. They were vastly different from each other. Some were sword carrying zealots. Some were fishermen. Some were brothers. All had quite different opinions about how to live out their destiny and to call on the Kingdom of God. They all needed approaching differently, all needed handling individually. When you study how the Lord dealt with them, look for the eight Cs consistently produced by Jesus. And when he had finally shown them that he would lay down his life for them. Not because he was forced to, but by his choice, they came into incredible harmony. Into such a unity that it changed the world!

Another key factor here that is being modelled by the Lord is the way that they all wanted to serve him. They all wanted the best for Him. When Peter cut off the ear of Malchus (John 18:10) he was not doing the will of the Lord, but he wanted to help! He was doing what he thought was best for the Lord and the Kingdom. It's so important that we acknowledge this about our parts so that we do not create disharmony by being angry, ashamed or fragmented around our parts' behaviour. Always remember that they are all trying to help!

What a lesson Jesus has left us. What a model to follow. But remember it took over three years of 24/7 care and commitment. Try your best not to be impatient with your 'selves' as you learn more about how they feel and how they are. Especially when what they feel is the best way forward doesn't seem to make sense to you. Over time, you will learn which parts have you acting out in extreme ways and why.

One of the main ways you can develop empathy for your parts is to remember that they are all you! They may be younger versions of you, they may not have your wisdom or understanding, they may not have your beliefs, but they are all parts of you, carrying your memories and experiences. They also carry God's spirit in the same way you do. Remember they all try to make good things happen. It is from this perspective and understanding that we can again approach Jesus' prayer in John 17. "I pray that they will all be one, just as you and I are one—as you are in me, Father, and I am in you. And may they be in us so that the world will believe you sent me".

How you recognise your parts behaviour

Your brain 'takes over' when it perceives a threat to be present. Remember, this is always done in an attempt to help you. However, your brain defines help as survival, so, if you are still breathing at the end of the day your brain is quite happy with the job that it's done, even if you have been placed in a desperate situation because of its strategies.

I help my clients to recognise their parts by these three things I mentioned previously in the section on Luke 15 when we looked at the 'prodigals' parts thinking. Remember, your parts will offer strategies that are **naive, radical** and **immediate**. (Does this sound like the Disciples to you)? Basically, they often think like children. Most traumatic experiences take place in childhood because the younger the child the easier they are to traumatise. Expect most of your parts to be quite young. Always look for these three factors in your triggered moments.

Immediate - Your parts are all about 'now' (no timeline). They won't care about tomorrow morning!

Radical - If a child learns that an adult is not to be trusted they will probably stop trusting all adults.

Naive - Your parts will not show anything approaching wisdom, it's all about survival.

This relates to trauma and what we've learnt about trauma in recent years. One of the main things being that human beings are complex! I often say to my clients that when we say 'I' we are using a complex statement. The fact is that as a human being you have many parts. Those parts are natural and are not part of a mental condition but part of the human condition. Years ago, I couldn't have written these words without you thinking that you were suffering from some kind of mental illness. It used to be called multiple personality disorder. In serious cases today it's still known as dissociative disorder. But for all the rest of us it's just called normal.

Over the last decade I have had many clients sit on my couch and say, "I'm going crazy". I explain to them after hearing about the situation that they're certainly not going crazy but rather are having a sane reaction to an insane situation. Sometimes it's about the way that they are reacting to something that makes them think they're crazy. Sometimes it's the way that they are contradicting themselves in their opinions and their behaviour.

I often ask them what football team they support. This is my simple way of helping them understand the complexity of being a human. Once they tell me their team, I tell them I support a different team. Then I ask this question. "Does this seem crazy"? Of course it doesn't! There are simply two opinions and two people in the same room. The confusion starts when two opinions are seen to come from one source.

It's because you think of yourself as **one thing** that causes the problem. Our imagination works separately (autonomously) from our mind, we all know this! There would be no architecture or poetry, no music or literature if everything had to be worked out consciously, one step at a time. We have all had 'eureka' moments when our imagination has delivered a solution that we did not work out consciously. This is how it is with our human experience. So how does this neuroscience 'discovery' relate to the Bible and the idea of discipling?

From conflict to harmony

Ask yourself this. What did Jesus do? He took a rag tag group of diverse individuals who all had different agendas. Then he turned them into a team that was completely unified in their commitment and purpose. He did this through his patience, teaching, disciplining and ultimately, his sacrifice. He committed to them, and they became willing to die for him.

Notice that none of the disciples had anything like the wisdom of the Lord. They all seemed more immature, and they certainly didn't understand the big picture. There were times when they acted in a way that frustrated Jesus (Mark 7:18). Times when he had to reverse their actions (John 18:11). And a lot of times where they seemed to disagree with the way that he wanted to go (Matthew 16:22).

This incredible experience and teaching concluded with the disciples finally acknowledging who he was following his death and resurrection. As they acknowledged him as their Lord and Saviour, they all became transformed and joined together in complete unity. Gone was the argumentative (Luke 9:46). Gone was the lack of confidence (Luke 18:26). Gone was the fear (Matthew 8:27). Gone was the doubting (John 20:25). Gone was the ego (Matthew 20:21). They were in harmony, and they were one. In acknowledging Jesus and seeing Him as the only way forwards, they lost all fear. They become unified and motivated to do the work of the Kingdom.

There are many accounts of how this unity played out in their lives, some more reliable than others. But there is no greater evidence of this unity than their deaths. Because they knew the truth and could not deny it, they were all martyred. Except John who was made immune from the poison that was forced upon him. He lived the life of a martyr on the Island of Patmos. This is how we believe they all died.

James died by the sword ordered by Herod Acts 12:2
Peter was crucified (upside down) in Rome
Andrew was hanged from an Olive tree in Patrae in Achaia
Thomas (known as doubting Thomas) was 'thrust through with pine spears'
Philip was tortured and crucified by angry Jews in Phrygia
Matthew was beheaded at Nav-Davar
Nathaniel was flayed and crucified
James (the lesser) was thrown from the top of the Temple in Jerusalem
Simon the zealot was crucified by the governor in Syria
Judas (not Iscariot) was beaten to death by pagan priests in Mesopotamia
Matthias (who replaced Judas Iscariot) was stoned whilst hanging from a cross in Ethiopia
John was not martyred but exiled to Patmos (although some reports say he was thrown into boiling oil)
Paul the Apostle was beheaded in Rome.

What produced this amazing level of discipline and commitment? An acceptance of Jesus as their Lord and Master. Total trust in Him. What was it that made that happen? Many things of course but it all started with receiving forgiveness.

No Condemnation

The disciples had been living under the law. As was everyone else. As the world still is. Since the time of Moses, they had been condemned by their sin and lived with the weight of this fact 24-7. Jesus showed them a separate way. Now that he was here, they would be living by faith and not under the law. That they were forgiven! This is as mind blowing today as it must have been then. In one fell swoop Jesus removed the power the Pharisees had over the people and offered everyone eternal life.

This was no small thing and is in fact the key that turns the lock both in discipleship and in your recovery. In John 8 we learn about the woman caught in the act of adultery and the way the Pharisees tried to trap Jesus by quoting Moses and the law. Jesus turned the tables on them and showed them the trap they were in! "Let he who is without sin cast the first stone" he said, and they all walked away. Finally, he said to the woman that he did not condemn her but told her to leave her life of sin.

In Luke 7 Jesus says directly to the woman who anoints him with oil "your sins are forgiven" and the guests are deeply shocked. In verse 49 we read that; The other guests began to say among themselves, "Who is this who even forgives sins?" I believe that this picture of forgiveness, discipling and harmony is at the very heart of recovery and should be your aim in developing your recovery through your 'inner life'.

As well as looking at how the disciples died, how they lived is also fascinating in the context of this 'inner Disciplining' idea. When they were first brought into the team, they were all over the place! Variously squabbling and arguing amongst themselves. Fighting with others, asking to be given 'pride of place' next to Jesus. As well as denying Christ and deserting him. When Christ died and rose again, they became totally unified and of one purpose. They began their real job in life, the one intended for them by God.

Let me ask you now as a way of helping you track your progress. How close are you to forgiving yourself for the things you have done? For the way you have been? Or are you still hating those parts of you that have had you acting out in this way? If you want to learn a better way, you have to stop fighting yourself. Inner conflict inhibits learning, and without learning there can be no progress.

You will return to the Disciples and their experiences later as part of your practice. Before we get to the practice section there is one more thing I want to challenge you with, it's the true nature of sin.

What is sin?

> BUT WITH ME IT IS A VERY SMALL THING THAT I SHOULD
> BE JUDGED BY YOU OR BY ANY HUMAN COURT.
> IN FACT, I DO NOT EVEN JUDGE MYSELF.
>
> 1 CORINTHIANS 4:3

You may think you have sin sorted. At least in your understanding if not in your practice. It's simple right? God is good and the Devil is evil. Black and white. Jesus is the way the truth and the life, Satan is the Father of all lies. Therefore, we should hate and run away from everything sinful and move towards everything that is good. Well, sure, in principle. But there's a lot more to it. If it were really that simple God would not have sent his son to rescue us but rather abandoned us to our evil fate.

When we reflect more deeply on what sin really is we get a more useful idea. The dictionary defines sin as "an immoral act considered to be a transgression against divine law". So, sin is something that goes against God's law. How does it do that? We could get a bit circular and say, "because it's evil". But that doesn't get us very far.

I want you to think of sin as something more understandable. As something we cannot avoid. Let's take some examples from the disciples, although I'm sure you could add many examples from your own life. Ask yourself this; In John 18:10 when Peter cut off the ear of Malchus did he think he was doing an evil thing or a good thing? He clearly thought that things would work out better if he resisted what the guards were doing with force. Now, of course it was wrong, and Jesus brought him back in line immediately. The point is that Peter was **trying to make a good thing happen**.

In Matthew 20:21 did James and John or their mother think they were being evil when they asked if they could sit next to him left and right in the Kingdom? Again, it was clearly wrong and sinful, but Salome thought she was doing a good thing, at least for them. And of course, this is the point. Sin happens mainly when people put their interests before God's (which is what your brain does naturally). Described best in Luke 12:13 known as the parable of the rich fool. Jesus calls this greed and tells us to watch out for it, teaching us that life is more than the accumulation of things.

In Romans 14:23 Paul tells us that when we are in doubt then we are sinning because it does not come from faith. Does this fit your definition of sin as simply an evil thing? In Jeremiah 10 and verse 23 and 24 we are reminded that we are not capable of discerning the right rules for life, only God can do this. My point in these examples is not that they were **not sinful**, but rather that these actions were **well intentioned**. And this is the key point in developing your recovery through an improved relationship with yourself ('parts').

So rather than go into a deeper analysis of this idea I want to stop here and make the point relevant to your recovery. You need to understand that sin is an inevitable result of self-interest. And your brain is not only interested in you but cannot be anything else! You also need to understand that the part of you that does the sinning wants to make a good thing happen! Until you understand most sinful motivation this way you will not be able to take the vital step towards working with your 'parts'. You will continue to fight your parts in a battle that you will mostly lose. Your 'parts' are like anxious children left on their own. Having to come up with solutions. Needing a parent. Trying their best to make a good thing happen, but without any experience, wisdom or concern for the greater good. Just like the Disciples. Now let's remind ourselves what Jesus did with them.

So, how are you dealing with this view of your sinful nature? What is your relationship with your inner parts like? Are you hating them, hiding them, ashamed of them? Or are you working with them like Jesus did? If you are attending a modern style of Church, most of the teaching will probably be quoting a modern Bible translation. I have noticed that the more modern the translation the more 'fighting' the talk. Take this example from Galatians 5:17. The 'Good News' translation describes the relationship between the spirit and the flesh as 'being enemies' and the 'New Living' Translation says that they are 'constantly fighting each other'. The 'Voice' says that 'there is a constant battle raging between them'. Compare this with the King James translation that simply says that they are 'contrary, the one to the other' or most older versions which say that they are 'in opposition' with each other. Much more measured language.

What I am saying does not contradict what the Bible says but expands the understanding of the model Jesus supplied when he discipled sinners. This then helps us to see more subtle ideas of what exists naturally within you as a human being. You are going to use this idea to create harmony rather than conflict within yourself.

In Romans Chapter 7 Paul helps us to understand the true nature of sin.

> WHAT THEN SHALL WE SAY? THAT THE LAW IS SIN? BY NO MEANS! YET IF IT HAD NOT BEEN FOR THE LAW, I WOULD NOT HAVE KNOWN SIN. FOR I WOULD NOT HAVE KNOWN WHAT IT IS TO COVET IF THE LAW HAD NOT SAID, "YOU SHALL NOT COVET."
> ROMANS 7:7-8

Sin is produced by the law, and the law is produced by God. Notice Paul says that 'he', meaning his fleshly self, would not have even known it was wrong to sin if God had not described sin through his word! No wonder the world wants to rid itself of God! If the world could do this then there would be no law, and if there is no law then there is no sin! Make no mistake, this is why all that vitriol and corrosive hatred is reserved for God by the world at large. He is the only thing standing between them and a reckless freedom to do anything they want. Proverbs 29:18 says that without vision (God's word) the people cast off all restraint. If they can get rid of God, they can do what they want!

You have a brain that cares only for your survival and safety and nothing and no one else. This understanding will help you to see sin in a different light. In doing this you will be identifying with Jesus and become more Christ-like.

Remember when he saw the large crowd and was moved with great compassion because they were like sheep without a shepherd (Mark 6:34). He wasn't filled with horror at their sinful natures. In developing your spiritual nature, you are going to become more Christ-like and work with your own lost sheep. Now you need to understand how to use the model that Christ left us when he worked with his close disciples.

Let's now look at the case for using the Disciple's story and their relationship with Jesus as a model for inner discipling. I want to encourage you to study the relationship between Jesus and the disciples from this perspective. Take some time now to look at how he was with them. Notice that he never rejected them, even when they were 'acting out' or wrong. Even though he knew they were evil! (Matt 7:11) When you study your Bible from this perspective you will notice lots of things that you will be using later in the practice section.

Jesus's prayer for you and me

Having mentioned John 17 in the context of inner unity several times, I now want to be clear on what I mean by this. I believe that Jesus' work with the Twelve disciples over those 3 years, along with many other things, give us a picture of what was being referred to in Jesus's prayer in John 17. I love this chapter and when I read it, I always remind myself of the circumstances in which it happened. After the last supper and before He was taken by the Soldiers to be crucified. This is important because it is the last opportunity on earth for Jesus to pray for himself, his disciples and his church before He was taken up to heaven.

Ask yourself another important question now. If you had one chance, one opportunity to pray for someone. What would you pray for? Of course, when I ask this question, I get a variety of answers. The point I want to get across is that it would probably be the most important prayer you could think of! I think we can safely assume that this prayer would be what the Lord considered to be the most important thing. It's the third section of the Chapter we are most interested in as he is praying for you and me! (John 17:20)

So, what does he pray for? He is just about to be taken and crucified! Let me ask you again. If you had one last chance to pray for people what would your prayer be? What does Jesus pray for as the most important thing? Is it that we should build a massive Church? No. Is it that we should go out and win millions of people for Him? No. Is it that we should have a great looking church building with great lighting, great sound and a top worship leader? No. Is it that we should spend all day reading the Bible? No. His prayer for you includes none of these things.

He prays for your unity, and I have been assured that the word that is used in the Bible comes from a root word that would translate just as well as the word 'harmony'. Now most of you will know this already and so you may be saying, "nothing new here for us". The thing I want to explore here is the type of unity that is being prayed for and how to achieve it. Those of you who have heard several messages about church and group unity may be in for a surprise.

We can naturally think of this prayer as being about 'group harmony' and take the whole third section of Chapter 17 to mean how we must all get on with each other. Especially in the Church, right? This would then fit with ideas like how the world will recognise us as disciples. That we love one another (John 13:35). I'm sure you have heard many sermons on this very idea. But is that the thing being suggested here? We can best understand the Bible by using the Bible and Jesus immediately goes on to describe the route we need to take to produce the type of harmony he is meaning and exactly what it should look like. He says, "as I am *in you,* and you abide *in me*". (My italics) Clearly showing that **inner harmony** is the intention, and 'outer harmony' is created through 'inner harmony'.

Let's look at another example. In Matthew 12 verse 22 onwards Jesus is explaining that any house divided against itself cannot stand. Once again, this can sometimes be described as getting on with each other, but in verse 26 he goes on to show us the context by using the example of Satan being divided against **himself**. Once again clearly defining inner unity or harmony as the thing that holds everything else together.

For me this is the vital point and one I want you to consider carefully, as it will guide your actions and attitude from now on. Given the examples Jesus uses and the prayer he makes for us, we can see the importance of our relationship with ourselves. Effectively Jesus was saying that inner harmony is the most important thing we can achieve. I believe that this is because everything we do and everything we achieve is produced from our inner state (Proverbs 10:11).

If inner harmony is what produces your life, you need to know how to achieve this without falling back into the trap of success and failure. You need a totally unique way of thinking about yourself that is not shaped by the medical model. The amazing truth is that God has already given us this approach in the way that his son Jesus worked with the disciples. Or, put another way, how your spirit should work with your flesh. Yes, that's right, I said work **with** your flesh! To help you understand how this will work, let's first understand more of the two aspects of your internal life, your mind and your brain.

Understanding the relationship between your mind and your brain

So how can you use this model to support your growth? First you need to understand the relationship between your brain and your mind. Your flesh and your spirit. This will show you a better way your mind and brain can relate to each other. Here are a few facts to include in your understanding.

Firstly, your life is (largely) being run by your adult (your consciousness, or what we call your 'core' self) but only on license from your brain! Your brain will 'take over' whenever it perceives enough threat. A threat to your life, your identity, your family, your rights, or your territory, will 'trigger' you. Often evoking a strong emotional reaction of anger, resentment, or fear. The more severe the threat, the more likely your brain will call the 'emergency services' of fight, flight flock or freeze into action. Your brain will then take over and decide which of these options is most likely to help you survive the threat. This will go on until your brain is convinced that the threat is over.

Do not be shocked at the idea that your conscious mind is shut down by your brain. This is a particularly useful part of the way you have been designed. Imagine for a moment that the fire alarm goes off in the building you are in. Which part of you would you like to help you survive? Your mind, which must work everything out, reflects on things, may be distracted by things like a favourite photo or even something like hunger! Or would you prefer your basic brain helped you, which is lightning fast, assesses the situation for the best way of surviving in an instant and provides the best chemical state for that course of action, is not in the least bit concerned with valuables and other distractions, and even knows how to shut down your appetite while you are escaping! There's no contest there. The brain wins every time. Of course, it's a trick question as it's not a real choice. The brain simply takes over when it perceives a threat to you.

All well and good then. This seems to work out fine. The problem arises when your brain perceives something to be a threat when it isn't! Something that was a threat when you were a child may still be 'stored' in the brain as a threat even though it isn't any more. What's worse, you've probably forgotten what happened and have not thought about it for years, and so have no idea why you are reacting this way.

Secondly, there is nothing unnatural about having 'parts' of us. Please do not think of this as a mental condition, rather it is the human condition! We have been designed this way. Did you ever wonder about the language God uses in Genesis 1:26? "Let us make man in our own image". Why the plurals? It's the trinity, right? We know about the Father, Son and Holy Spirit as being three in one and we talk about this all the time, but do we explore the ramifications of this? If we are made in God's image, then we are like Him. Multifaceted, with various parts doing different jobs. The problem is not that you have different opinions of what to do next and different voices going on in your head. The problem is not that you are ill, the problem is that you are not in 'unity'.

Thirdly, your mind cannot overpower or shut down your brain, but your brain can shut down your mind whenever it feels the need to. I say to my clients that "your mind runs your life…… on licence from your brain!" This is one of the main reasons my approach is not based on fighting problems but outgrowing them. Attempting to overpower your brain or demand that it does what you want it to puts you in conflict with yourself. This usually leads to your brain's resistance being made stronger!

Science catching up with the Bible

> For, "Who has known the mind of the Lord so as to instruct him?" But we have the mind of Christ.
>
> 1 Corinthians 2:16

Never have we understood so well the way the brain works and particularly the relationship between the brain and the mind. Think of your mind as a small part of your brain that is conscious and has a moral centre. It is the 'frontal lobes', the filter through which everything must pass. The way you make meaning and decide things. Even now as you are reading this!

The brain on the other hand is best thought of as your engine room. Behind the scenes, your brain is running and checking many systems, regulating pressures and flow, temperature and efficiency in ways I am not anywhere near qualified to describe. I know that it does this 24/7 without ever sleeping or without you knowing about it. Your brain does not care about most of the decisions that you are making during the day. Decisions like what jumper should I wear today, or which sandwich should I choose for my lunch. But there are some things that alert your brain to 'get involved'.

Think of the relationship between your brain and your mind like that of licensing. Your life is being run by your mind on licence from your brain. That licence can be revoked in a few thousands of a second if the brain becomes aware of a threat to you. We all acknowledge that the brain is running so much of our lives behind the scenes. It is amazing what it does without our knowledge and without any conscious understanding, running many systems in your body simultaneously.

So, when does your brain 'take over' and why would your brain do this? Well, the 'why' is easy, the part of the brain we are talking about operates on threat so we could say that it takes over to help you to survive. It does so based on information received from your senses as well as the knowledge stored from your experience, and it does so at lightning speed. In any practical evaluation we could say the takeover is immediate.

Have you ever been walking along behind someone in a wooded area and a branch or leaves flick back at you as they walk ahead? Before your conscious mind knew what was happening your brain saw the threat, shut down your mind, took over, closed your eyes, lowered your head and lifted your arm! This was all before your conscious mind knew what was happening! Clearly, we need this protection. Remember your brain is far faster and will take over any time it perceives a threat.

So, this is necessary and part of your design. However, the brain does not distinguish between real and perceived threats, it simply operates on the information you give it. Like a computer, it works on the information you type in. That's why when you watch a film, the emotions your brain (back room) delivers are absolutely real even though your mind (front room) is perfectly aware that it's just a film. Your brain does not distinguish very well between what's real and what is perceived. A computer does not ask "is this information 'real'?" This can be quite inconvenient not just when you're watching emotionally moving films but when something appears to be a threat to your brain but is not threatening at all to your adult self. This reaction from your brain is called 'triggering'.

Let's take a quick look at what God did with us as a way of explaining this. He first gave us a set of rules to live by. These were called the Ten Commandments. Following these commands is a bit like the mind trying to overpower or rule the brain. What happened? You may recall things didn't turn out so well. In fact, it went so badly that He decided that this could not be corrected and had to start all over again by drowning the lot of us. From that time on the world was being prepared for Jesus to come and be sacrificed for our sins.

When he came and fulfilled scripture through his life, death and resurrection he first worked with disciples and prepared them to work with him rather than against him as the pre-Noah lot had done. It is this harmony that is so necessary in your recovery. Do not try to force your brain to obey you. If you have been trying to do this you need to pause. First understand the way your brain works, then understand the nature of what threatens it, and finally you need to work with those 'parts' that have been trying to protect you and create unity and harmony in your inner life. This is the process of 'inner discipling'.

CHAPTER FOUR

Jesus and His Disciples

> FOR EVER SINCE THE WORLD WAS CREATED, PEOPLE HAVE SEEN THE EARTH AND SKY. THROUGH EVERYTHING GOD MADE, THEY CAN CLEARLY SEE HIS INVISIBLE QUALITIES — HIS ETERNAL POWER AND DIVINE NATURE. SO THEY HAVE NO EXCUSE FOR NOT KNOWING GOD.
>
> ROMANS 1:20

One of the things that Paul is trying to get across in the letter to the Romans quoted above is that as well as reading his word, there is at least one more way of knowing, acknowledging, and learning about God. We only have to look at the design, and the way things work to see our creator. Paul says that this is so clear that we can have no excuse for not knowing God! We could include things like in Proverbs six and verses six to eleven where we are asked to consider the ant! Or we could use the birds (Matt 6:26) or even the flowers (Matt 6:28). In verse twenty of Romans 1 he refers to what everyone can see for themselves. In fact, he is saying that they cannot avoid seeing it! He talks about the earth and the sky as things that 'clearly' make known to us Gods 'eternal power and divine nature'.

I want to be clear about the idea that in our approach to personal spiritual growth we will be using what we see to develop our method. If I was to ask you about Jesus' ministry, what would you say it was? Of course, he came to suffer and die for the sins of many, but what did he actually do? Let's remind ourselves that his main ministry time was spent discipling. Teaching correcting and connecting with a set of individuals and making them into a team that became closer than disciples. A team that became friends (John 15:15). We are going to take this idea and apply it personally.

Jesus had many Disciples, not just twelve. We have all heard about them in Sermons and read about them. Jesus taught them over a period of about three years. I am going to invite you to take a fresh look at this process, not just as ministry work, but as a wonderful example of how to view and manage ourselves. **Not to replace** any of the teaching about discipling you already know, but to add to your understanding by seeing their lives and experiences with Jesus as a model for your own growth and development. Your journey into recovery.

Following the Bible

We all try to follow the Bible. Its teachings, its truth and its author. Psalm 3 says that we should not 'lean on our own understanding'. As well as living by the Bible's instruction, we can also live by using God's design and God's ways. We see His design all around us in the way He structures things like the seasons and resting on the seventh day which is a principle built into the land and used by Farmers as they leave their fields fallow to allow them to regain their nutrients before being planted again.

This principle is well known and stretches from Solomon saying that 'there is a season for everything' in Ecclesiastes. The way the Universe has been designed shows us God's power and creativity. His design also offers us directions on how to live. We learn about God, not just from his word, but through his design! Whether it's the seasons, time, or the things Jesus did when he walked the earth.

So, we are following a God inspired route if we can think of the methods Jesus used with the Disciples not only as examples of leadership and inspiration for our ministry with others, but also as a model for how we should work with our 'inner self'. By using Jesus' relationship with the Disciples as a model for our own individual growth, we have a proven way of utilising the truth of God's word to further God's Kingdom through the development of our own recovery.

We are going to take the idea of discipling (Jesus and the twelve) and use it as our internal model of growth and harmony. But just to make it perfectly clear that I am not asking you to replace 'discipling' as it is presented in the Bible, I will first talk about the difference between the two, especially the way that internal discipling does not disqualify external discipling. I hope this will remove any issues you may have about using this method.

CHAPTER FIVE

Inner and Outer discipling

> Pointing to his disciples, he said,
> "Here are my mother and my brothers.
>
> Matthew 12:49

I want to now make clear, the distinction between inner and outer discipling. Jesus had twelve main disciples, He discipled them over a three-year period and later they went out into the world and changed everything. You and I are only Christians because of what they did. So, we have a pattern which we call 'discipling', which, after completing this book you might begin to call 'outer discipling'. Fine, we have a great model to follow, and we should follow it to the best of our ability.

I am in no way contradicting this model. But what if the way the Lord worked with the disciples also gave us an inner pattern as well as an external or outer pattern? If we reproduced this same model, the model of Jesus with twelve disciples internally as well as externally? What would that look like?

Picture Jesus with the twelve disciples under him. Now reproduce that whole picture again inside each disciple.

It is from this perspective that we can develop a working model. A coherent way of approaching those parts of us that, like the disciples, often have such a mistaken idea of what is helpful. This is the idea that you will be working with as part of this program. It is an approach that will build your recovery through personal growth. By producing inner harmony without fighting, hating, denying or exiling parts of yourself.

In taking the twelve disciples and working with them Jesus not only gave us a model of discipling that we can follow and practice with others. He also provided a model of inner harmony and growth by modelling how we should relate to our 'inner selves' or parts. How he taught and developed them. How he related to them. How he disciplined them but never rejected them. How he was patient with them. These lessons offer us God's way of working with our inner parts. Now where does this 'work' take place?

Outer Discipling

There are essentially two forms of the discipling pattern. The one we all know about is like a photocopier, reproducing itself through the copying process. This is what I am calling 'outer discipling'. As we share the good news and welcome people into the love of God, we work to reproduce in others how we were converted. In this way the mass or 'amount' of the pattern increases as the Kingdom grows.

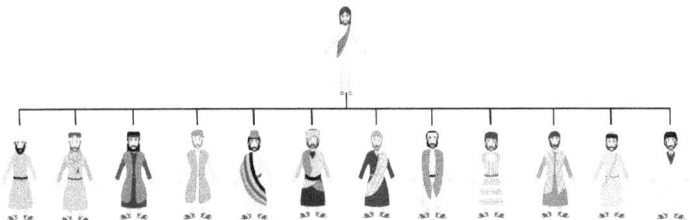

Jesus teaches the 12 Disciples

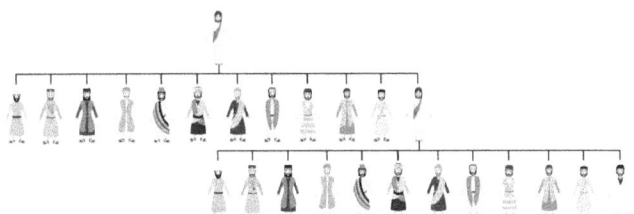

Each Disciple produces more disciples

Inner Discipling

To produce growth through inner harmony you can develop the second form which is what I am calling 'inner discipling'. In this form you replicate the whole pattern inwardly, including Jesus and the other disciples or 'parts' of you, 'within' yourself. The difference between these two forms of repeating patterns is the difference between 'inner discipling' and 'outer discipling'.

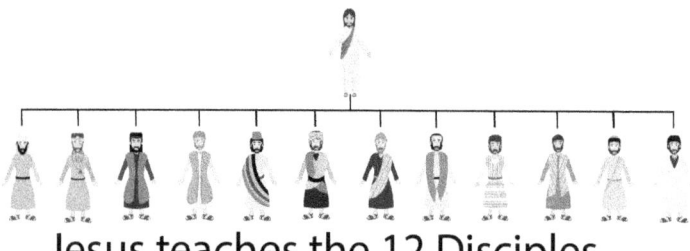

Jesus teaches the 12 Disciples

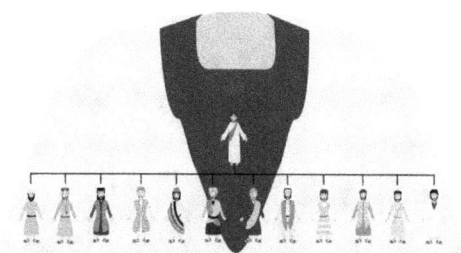

Each Disciple reproduces the pattern internally

The Bible as internal and external guidance

This idea of using the (outer) discipling relationship between Jesus and his disciples as an (internal) tool to help with personal growth and spiritual development can be taken further. Imagine for a moment the Old Testament as external and the New Testament as internal. I have found it to be an extremely useful study. The Old Testament is full of battles in which many people died. Temples were rebuilt. God appeared in burning bushes. Daniel walked through real fires. In the New Testament, the battle is internal, with our flesh. Jesus tells us that our bodies are now the temple, and God appears within us by sending his holy spirit. The fires we walk through are mainly the 'refining fires' that sharpen us for ministry.

I'm not presenting this idea as fact. I am fully aware that the persecuted church is going through things that are painfully real. Rather, I am presenting it as a fascinating way to study and learn from the Bible. In this book we will not only be talking about 'inner discipling', but also things like the 'upper room' as something you can understand internally.

The quality of your state determines the quality of your work

The first question I tend to face when I propose this 'internal/external idea to people is "what use is it if it does not increase the Kingdom"? My argument is simple and is backed up many times in scripture. What you do externally is produced by your internal state. In Matthew 7 Jesus describes false prophets as appearing to be sheep but inwardly being ferocious wolves. Going on to say that a good tree cannot bear bad fruit and a bad tree cannot bear good fruit. Unless you work to become a good tree, you will always be working in vain and working against yourself. If you do not acknowledge this, you may always be working at a disadvantage no matter how good your intentions are. The most effective work you do outside of yourself will be determined by the work you do inside yourself.

When we think of becoming disciples there are lots of sermons and teachings about this. Mainly the instruction is practical and involves 'outer discipling'. How we behave and interact with others. 'Winning people to Christ' is the main outcome of discipling but how is it achieved? I am arguing that it is best achieved through first doing the work of 'inner discipling'.

Of course, there is a lot of instruction on our 'inner life' in the Bible. How we think and how our beliefs govern our actions (Matthew 6:21). We are told that the way we think is important and that it should be 'renewed' (Romans 12:2). We are reminded that our thinking is the cause of most of our problems (James 4:1). We are taught to 'take every thought captive' (2 Corinthians 10:5). But how many of you have heard a sermon telling you exactly how to do this? If you have, I can almost guarantee that the teaching will have led to you forming another 'inner conflict', with emphasis on the battle you are in and how to 'win it'. Generally, these teachings are constructed using the medical model, which usually leads you straight back into a battle with yourself.

The flesh and the spirit

To help you make sense of this approach and use it to grow and make progress, I now want to explain the way to think about your inner life and workings. There are many ways to understand this. Terms like your brain, mind, and unconscious, not to mention the soul, spirit and the flesh! In this approach we will be simplifying things down to mind and brain (spirit and flesh) so that we can do two things. Firstly, to help us focus on what we are wanting to use. Secondly, as a way of comparing the spiritual terms with the psychological terms you may be more familiar with. I have found it immensely helpful in my work to match up the psychological terms with the more Biblical and spiritual terms we will be using.

Here is a graphic to help you see how you can compare the terms we often use, with the equivalent spiritual terms, as a way of understanding them. All these terms finally drill down to the brain and the mind. This graphic is to help you understand how to think of yourself and how science is now catching up with the Bible. We start with the big divide, that is the world and the kingdom of God. In John 18:36, Jesus says "My kingdom is not of this world. If it were, my servants would fight to prevent my arrest by the Jewish leaders. But now my kingdom is from another place."

Once we interpret the world and the kingdom of God as being the difference between the flesh and the spirit, we can then go further and see the disciples as the flesh and Jesus as the spirit. Finally, we can 'internalise' this and understand this divide as the brain and the mind. As we approach the practice part of the book, I want you to think of your mind as your spirit and your brain as the flesh. This view will help you to understand why you are so often in conflict with yourself.

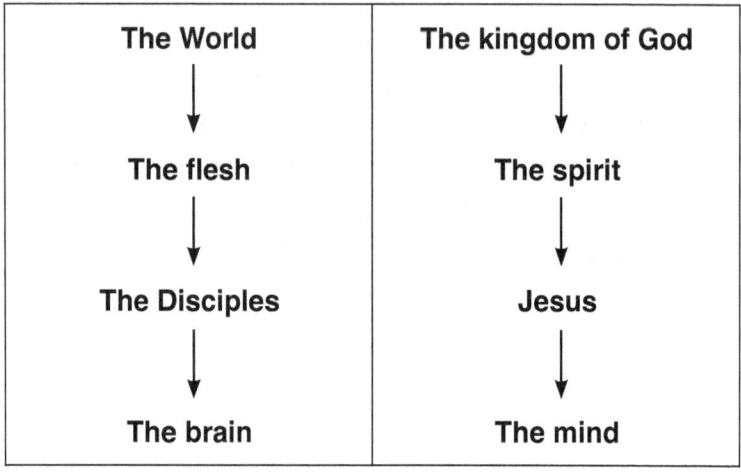

Reading this from the top we have the various comparisons, starting with the biggest example which is the world with the Kingdom of God. As we move down the table the examples become smaller and more focussed to the point where we arrive at the brain and the mind. The world is the same as the flesh and the Disciples are flesh. The spirit is Jesus and when He lives in you, He resides in your mind. Using this distinction, we arrive at our innermost selves.

To understand the Biblical nature of this approach we first needed to make a clear distinction between the medical view and the Biblical view of yourself as a human being. As part of this understanding, we took a fresh look at the true nature of sin. We also encouraged you to see the value of the harmonised self over the conflicted self. But before you can practice effectively, you still need one more thing. You need to understand what is meant by 'triggering' or the flesh reaction to threat. So, what do we mean by 'triggering'?

CHAPTER SIX

Triggering

> NOW IF I DO WHAT I DO NOT WANT TO DO,
> IT IS NO LONGER I WHO DO IT, BUT IT
> IS SIN LIVING IN ME THAT DOES IT.
>
> ROMANS 7:20

This is a term you may not have heard before so let me first explain what it is. Remember, your mind (conscious or core self) runs your life. But only on licence from your brain! This licence can be revoked at any time (in milliseconds), particularly if things go wrong. Any time your brain decides that you are threatened it will 'shut' you (your mind) down and take over. You may know this as the 'fight or flight' idea.

How does my brain get trained in these ways

This idea of your brain 'deciding' on whether you are threatened or not is governed by your life experiences. This is a key point because if you do not understand this, you will continue to think of yourself as broken and needing fixing. Your brain is assessing threat based upon your life experiences. These experiences have trained your brain to see certain things as threatening, and so when it reacts to protect you, it's just working really, really well! Because your brain is incredibly consistent, it will continue to think of these things as threatening until you retrain it.

The training is simply a matter of your brain seeing you follow the same thought/behaviour pattern repeatedly and storing it. Remember, your brain is watching everything you do and is constantly 'rewiring' itself to put this new learning into practice. In fact, this is great evidence that your brain is working well! It is quite brilliant at learning, storing the knowledge and reproducing it when the circumstances require it. Think about how many times and for how many years you have followed certain thought and behaviour patterns. Your brain has learned them all and stored them as threats to you!

Why is this so important? Remember that the front room (your mind) has a lot of sophistication, you will assess the level of threat in very subtle ways. Your back room (the brain) simply has an 'on' and 'off' switch! If you train your brain that this 'thing' is a threat it will assume you are going to die if it does not protect you. Think 'animal in the jungle' and you get the idea. There is no subtlety here! Your brain takes your safety very seriously.

When we watch a film, we (that is our minds) know perfectly well that we are watching actors and lights, cameras and scripts. But the feelings we have are real! These films can make us jump out of our skins, become anxious, laugh or cry. So, whilst your brain is incredibly complex it's also easily fooled! The best way to think about this is to see your brain as a computer which receives information. When you tap letters and numbers into your computer, the computer never asks if the information is 'real' or 'imaginary'. Your input is simply understood as information.

It is this perspective the flesh (brain) has about what is truly important that Jesus spoke about a lot. Take Matthew 10 and verse 28 where Jesus says "Do not be afraid of those who kill the body but cannot kill the soul. Rather, be afraid of the One who can destroy both soul and body in hell". Your brain is designed to protect you from threats to your body and works on caution. If you are still breathing at the end of the day, your brain will feel that it has done its job. This is why your brain can bring thoughts and strong compulsions to do things that are unhealthy or downright risky. Following years of training where you have shown your brain what your solution looks like, it learns to offer you that same solution every time the 'bad thing' happens. If this training did not happen, we would only react based upon 'real' threats and dangers.

So, you are triggered when your brain perceives you to be threatened. At this point your brain 'shuts down' your mind and takes over. Who you think of as 'you' is not always in charge of your life. As you learn more about how you are triggered and what triggers you, you may be shocked to find just how much time you spend in a triggered state and how long you remain in that state. You are going to learn how to use your experience of these threats and triggered states to grow into your recovery and make progress.

Radical, immediate and naive

When you first start to look for examples of triggering in your life, look out for these three things. **Radical, immediate and naive**. Your brain (parts or disciples) will always show these tendencies in its approach and attitude. This can often appear childlike or just plain inexperienced. There are many examples of this in the disciples' lives. Matthew 26 and verse 22 is one of the most well-known. Peter takes out his sword and chops off the ear of Malchus. If you look at this from just about any perspective, it doesn't make sense and Jesus corrects him. Peter's actions are radical, immediate and naive! Or take John chapter 9 and verse 54. Here James and John ask Jesus if he wants them to call down fire from heaven to destroy a Village just because they did not welcome Jesus! About as radical and naive as it gets.

It will not take you long to find examples of this attitude in your life. You will start to notice attitudes when triggered that do not look, sound or act like 'you'. How many times have you heard yourself say "I don't know what came over me". When you see this in yourself make sure that you do not judge or hate these things, rather get interested in what it is that caused your brain to feel that you were threatened. Is there any history here that you recognise? Okay, time to understand triggering a little deeper.

The four stages of triggering

I want you to think of this idea of triggered states and your brain taking over as an opportunity for inner discipling. There are four main ways in which we can identify triggered states and I will show you examples of all four from the Bible as well as explaining them. As you become more aware of yourself and the way your flesh and your spirit are often in conflict, you will start to identify certain parts with certain disciples. Giving your parts names is a common therapeutic technique since, to achieve integration we must first employ separation (this is so that we know what it is we are integrating). To achieve harmony, we must first address the conflict. There are four main triggered stages, chemical (feelings), mental (thoughts), verbal (words) and behavioural (actions).

In Matthew 26 we see all four states. First, we see Peter in a grandiose triggered state in verse 33 he says that even if these others fall away I never will. Then in verse thirty-five Peter and the others declare that they will die before disowning Jesus. This is the third triggered stage, verbal. This is not their authentic selves talking. Later Peter denies knowing Jesus because he is afraid for his life, but Jesus told him not to be afraid of people who could only take his life, but to fear the one who could take life and soul! (Matt 10:28). In verse 70 and 72 Peter is in the third stage when he denies Jesus with his words. But it's in verse 26 that we see the fourth stage of triggering, when they all deserted him, they ran away. Now I will go through the stages, one at a time.

The first trigger - Chemical

The first and most basic way we can recognise when we are triggered is chemical. We feel different. It might be a turning of the stomach, it might be a tension in the throat, it may be a tightening of the chest, or downright terror! The main thing to be aware of is that you will feel quite different, very quickly, and that this reaction will be out of proportion. You haven't just changed the way you feel, you have experienced a younger part of you, their feelings and the inexperienced beliefs that produced them. If you don't intervene at this stage, you may experience the second stage.

The second trigger - mental

The second triggering stage is mental. Rather than believing yourself to be thinking differently, think of yourself as literally thinking the thoughts of the part. And it's not just thoughts themselves, this change of state will include the beliefs and agenda of that part of you. If this part of you is very young, it will be obvious to you that your attitude has shifted when triggered at this level. As you understand this better and learn to work with this model you will get to know your parts much better. If you do not intervene at this stage, you may experience the third level of triggering.

The third trigger - verbal

If you are triggered at this level, you will find yourself using the words, vocabulary and speech patterns of the part. It's at this stage where we are likely to be interacting with others which often leads to us saying "I lost my head" or "I don't know what came over me". Watch for your speech pattern becoming slower and deeper if it's a depressed part. Or faster, louder and higher in pitch if it's an angry part. Swearing may be something you only do when this part is around. It's in the thinking and talking that you will notice the difference between your 'core self' and the parts. You will look back and remember yourself saying things you do not actually believe, but your part does! If you do not intervene at this stage, you may experience the fourth level of triggering which is behavioural.

The Fourth trigger - behavioural

Triggering at the fourth level will involve 'acting' like the part. It's at this stage where most of the disasters happen. Extreme examples include excessive drinking or drug use, excessive gambling or starting an affair, but it could be something less noticeable like withdrawing or going quiet, isolating or even 'helping others'. It's when we 'act out' this way that we can see the difference between our parts and our true self most clearly. Remember, there is a much smaller spiritual dimension to your brain (parts), so the behaviour is often purely carnal (fleshly). You may be horrified by your thoughts, feelings and behaviour at these times. In your past this may have caused you to hide these things because of shame. Using this approach, you are going to learn to work with these things as Jesus worked with them.

Remember, all your parts are younger than you, some of them are much younger. They do not have your wisdom, maturity or life experience. Their ideas of what is the best thing to do may be staggeringly naive. Especially when compared with how you normally behave, and what you understand to be acceptable behaviour.

You may 'observe' yourself doing something and say, "why am I doing this"? Again, you may reflect later "I don't know what came over me." You may think that you are going crazy because you are doing things you do not want to do. You are now squarely at the point Paul was writing about in Romans 7:20 'Now if I do what I do not want to do, ***it is no longer I who do it***, but it is sin living in me that does it'. (My italics) I don't want to be too blunt about this, but could Paul have put it any clearer for us? He tells us, in black and white, that it's not him that did these things, but something else! This description of the triggered state should help you understand more about the nature of sin and the sinful (fleshly or brain) part of us.

The nature of the triggered self

> THE MIND GOVERNED BY THE FLESH IS HOSTILE TO GOD;
> IT DOES NOT SUBMIT TO GOD'S LAW, NOR CAN
> IT DO SO. THOSE WHO ARE IN THE REALM
> OF THE FLESH CANNOT PLEASE GOD.
>
> ROMANS 8:7/8

I want to be clear about one more thing here on the idea of triggering, which may help you to make sense of your experience. *When you are triggered, you are always outside the will of God.* Your 'parts' are of the flesh therefore they are always in opposition to God and cannot please Him. Remember that the flesh cannot understand God. Seriously, your brain has no idea what God is. You might as well try to explain God to a Cow in a field. As a result, whenever you are in a triggered state you can never be in the will of God (Romans 8:7). The important part of this scripture is the idea *'nor can it do so'*. Once you accept that your flesh cannot follow God's will, you are in the best position to work with your parts.

Certainty

As you start your harmonising work of inner discipling, you will quickly learn that all your parts are certain about something! They always have an agenda! They believe that this thing needs to happen, and it needs to HAPPEN NOW! Again, this is a useful way of learning to distinguish between your brain and your mind. In your mind you are often open-minded, or curious. Your brain rarely is. So, look for those times where you were not ready to compromise or accept any other interpretation.

Proportion

Because the brain is taking over based upon what it perceives to be a serious threat, the reaction will always be 'out of proportion'. Once you understand this, you will be able to assume that any out of proportion reaction is a triggered state, a 'part' of you, or, in other words, your brain has taken over. When you simplify things down to this level you will be able to practice very well since you will not mistake your Christ mindedness (mind or heart) with your inner disciples (Brain or flesh). When you read the Bible, you never mistake Jesus for the disciples! Once you have made a clear distinction between your parts and your core self you can begin to practice 'inner discipleship'.

Reactions and Responses

I want you to think of this difference between your mind and your brain as the difference between a response and a reaction. So, the responses come from your core self, and reactions come from your flesh or brain. What type of reaction you get is based upon the way life and your experiences have trained your brain. Learning, beliefs, and attitudes arising from events and circumstances have been fed into your brain for years and it has learned what you like and what you don't, as well as some of the solutions you have put in place.

Acceptance and rejection

This set of beliefs have been formed by what your younger self believed would make you unacceptable and what would make you acceptable. How to avoid rejection. Think of this as training. Your brain, which takes notice of everything you do, has learned from years of this and is continually using this training experience to help you as best it can by taking over when it perceives something to be a threat. So, these reactions are programmed in, they arise from the flesh (brain) and are lightning fast. Much too fast to control! Your responses on the other hand, which come from your mind (core self), are conscious, considered, and reflective. They come more from a moral sense of right and wrong and who you want to be. As Christians, we want to be more like Jesus.

We cannot stop reactions! We all have them.

When you have an 'out of proportion' reaction your practice is to turn it into a response as quickly as you can. In therapy, we call this 're-triggering' the adult. You do this by continually 'checking out' what you are thinking and feeling (especially when you get any sense that something is wrong) as part of your growth practice. This is called the 'observer position' and will be covered below as part of this section. When you feel that some part of your 'Christ mindedness' has dropped out, so start from a position of acceptance that this has happened. Once again there is no such thing as an 'unacceptable thought or feeling'. Remember that acceptance of something does not mean that it is correct, that you agree with it or that it is permanent, it just means that it is real! Better behaviour will naturally emerge from acceptance. Jesus always taught from a position of reality, accepting things as they were before correcting them.

By learning the true value of acceptance, you can shift from a reaction to a response as soon as possible. When we use the idea of acceptance, we take our psychological and emotional realities into the spiritual realm. This gives us a chance to produce something much more useful. I want to say a little more now on behaviour, which I regard as 'evidence of change.' If you have not realised it yet let me state it clearly. **We change from the inside** and so behaviour is evidence of internal change. I never work by telling someone to change their behaviour.

God given resources

> AND THE PEACE OF GOD, WHICH
> TRANSCENDS ALL UNDERSTANDING,
> WILL GUARD YOUR HEARTS AND YOUR MINDS IN CHRIST JESUS.
> PHILIPPIANS 4:7

In case you didn't get this yet, I want to be clear about something. The resources God has supplied you with are perfect! When the Bible says that the peace of God passes all understanding it means that there is no natural reason why we should experience such calm based on our lived experience. When we see God's people forgive those who have murdered their loved ones, we know we are seeing something supernatural, something that would never come from the flesh.

So, when we talk about calm, we mean perfect calm! It is so amazing to realise that Neuroscience testing has shown that we all have these resources no matter what our past has been like! If these resources come from God, then you would expect two things, firstly that they would be perfect, and secondly that they would be untainted by your lived experience. That is exactly what you will find when you practice the observer position.

When you employ these methods, along with taking the observer position, you are likely to 'retrigger' the authentic self. Although the 'part' may not 'step back' completely. After all, no one likes to give up power! You may initially experience something like a lessening of the feelings the part brings. This will allow you more options in your decision making and self-management. Even a small amount of success will change your experience of certain events or challenges.

It is not only life that triggers you. Your brain makes very little distinction between what is real and what is observed. Working only with the information it receives from your senses (when you watch a film the feelings you have are real even though you know that it's just actors reading a script). You can trigger yourself. This can become an extremely useful (and safe) exercise. Try sitting in a comfortable and safe place and start to think about the last time this extreme feeling happened. You may find that this is enough to trigger the feelings again, but maybe not as strong. Use this as an exercise as there is no better time to talk to your parts as when they are fully present. Keep checking that you are still curious about the parts feelings and ideas. If you lose your curiosity and start judging, take a break and start again later.

Once you achieve this observing state you can begin to develop a better relationship with your parts. Inner discipling begins when you recognise your parts as separate from yourself and relate to them as their Lord and master. Remember that we are trying to create inner harmony here or what could be called trust or acceptance of you as the leader. So, try to remain calm and friendly with all parts even if the progress is slow. If the 'parts' overwhelm you with contrary thoughts and ideas, see how much you can learn from the experience, forgive yourself and try again later with some of the approaches the Lord took with his disciples. Always trying to develop a better relationship with that part.

If you need to feel more 'yourself' or in control at any time, just ask yourself any question that begins with "I wonder…"? Such as "I wonder how I'm feeling now"? Or "I wonder how old this part is"? Any 'self-reflective' question like this will have the effect of waking you up as the authentic self is the only part of you that is interested in questions that include genuine curiosity. A more straight forward question such as, "how am I feeling now"? will not work since the part knows how it feels. You are likely to get an answer like "I'm angry, how do you think I feel"? Putting "I wonder" in front of the question places you in the observer position.

CHAPTER SEVEN

Producing harmony instead of conflict

The fact that there is often more than one opinion in your mind doesn't mean you're going crazy. It means that you are a normal human being. Have you ever said to yourself "I'm in two minds about that" or "there's a part of me that doesn't want to do this"? Did you ever say, "I lost my head"? As soon as we recognise the reality of our complex nature, we have made a vital step towards the way we're going to grow and develop as a person, which will be our route to personal growth.

As a Christian I believe that God gives us all kinds of examples. Things that are woven into creation and design tell us about his nature. Whilst these things tell us about the nature of God, they also tell us about ours since we are made in his image. When we read Genesis 1:26 we find an extraordinary idea. The idea that God's nature is multiple. when he says "let us make man in our own image" this is not Moses making a typo. God is revealing to us his multifaceted nature and as we are made in his image, we share that multiple nature.

So, what does this mean for the way we think about ourselves? Personally, I can't imagine doing any therapy work now that does not include this idea of the complex self. I would go as far as to say that any therapeutic approach that does not include the idea of the multifaceted nature of the human being is going to fall short. That's not to say that other approaches don't work or never work. Of course they do, but the reason they work is because the process of getting your brain to trust you is a natural one, sometimes achieved without you knowing it. The approach I am taking in this book simply offers you the most direct route to achieving that trust as part of yourself management and growth.

Your parts are natural in that they are designed to be there. We all know about the main two reactions of the brain: **fight** and **flight**, right? You may not be so familiar with the '**flocking** and **freezing**' parts. These parts include strong states of anger, sadness and fear. Without which it becomes exceedingly difficult to function in the world. If the building you are in is on fire your brain is much better equipped to get you out than your mind. If your family is threatened, you need to get angry. If your safety is threatened, you need to be afraid. Problems arise not because you have parts, but because they have been trained **through your experience** to think of things as threatening that are no longer threatening to you as an adult. So, parts develop roles that are constructed through our experience.

As children we learn what is acceptable and what is rejectable through our parents' attitude. The child psychologists tell us that as young children we are well aware that we will die if we do not receive the approval of our caregivers. Basically, to your brain, acceptance means life and rejection means death. That is how serious your brain takes the idea of threats. So, these parts constructed through trauma are essentially **natural parts** being asked to play **unnatural roles**.

When you think of threats, just look at the huge spectrum of ideas you have in your mind. Everything from someone slighting you or looking at you the wrong way, all the way up to someone trying to kill you! You need to understand that your brain does not have anything as sophisticated as this spectrum. Think of it more like a light switch, it's either on or it's off. That's why it takes these so-called threats so seriously, it's always life or death, with nothing in between.

Inner harmony rather than inner conflict

> I CARE VERY LITTLE IF I AM JUDGED BY YOU OR BY ANY HUMAN COURT; INDEED, I DO NOT EVEN JUDGE MYSELF.
>
> 1 CORINTHIANS 4:3

Remember where we started in John 17? Jesus' prayer for us is outer harmony created through 'inner harmony' so any method that produces inner conflict is on the wrong path. Inner conflict is created when you start to hate 'part of you' or start to fight with 'part of you' because of what it has you doing or saying. Because fighting with ourselves leads us down the wrong path this often leads to disaster. I will return to this subject later as part of the problem that often occurs within the Church but for now, I will talk about this issue as I face it every day in my counselling work.

When I first describe this model to an addicted client, particularly a Christian client they are shocked and often frightened. They often say something like "I'm fighting this thing every day with everything I've got, and you are saying stop fighting it"! Or something like "It's only my efforts in fighting it off that is keeping this thing at bay. If I stop fighting, I'll be in real trouble". This can be incredibly challenging to think about if you have believed that you have been in line with the Bible's teaching when you fight like this. Getting over this 'battling' idea is often the most challenging part of their recovery. Remember earlier when I spoke about western culture being "saturated in the medical model"? Remember, the medical model 'pathologises' our 'parts' whilst the Church often 'demonises' them. Either way they are seen as external to our 'selves' and something to be fought off or prayed away.

Your parts are trying to help you

I want to offer another approach. I will be describing what I mean by our 'parts' or 'inner disciples' in detail later but first I want to turn one massive ship around. I want you to know that all these parts are trying to make a good thing happen. They are not external demons or problems. They are all parts of you, and they are trying to make a good thing happen. They may be mistaken, naive, egotistical or just plain dumb. But they are trying to help. They are not trying to screw up your life or make things worse.

Did you ever question someone's attempt to help you? Did someone's attempt to make things better ever go wrong?

Did you ever wish they had left things as they were? Of course, you have. And here's another question for you. Do any of these things remind you of the disciples' efforts to 'help'? Remember, they wanted a leader that would attack the Romans and defeat them. Jesus didn't say fight them, he said to pray for them. This idea was just as confusing to the disciples as it may be to you now.

Covering as a strategy of your parts

We have all seen a set of Russian dolls. These are amazing as they all sit inside one another. I am probably not alone when I say that there always seemed to me to be something profound about this idea. I use a set of these dolls when working with clients as I try to explain the construction and role of our parts, and I think it would be useful to include this idea now.

If you have studied any of the excellent books on the IFS approach, you will no doubt be familiar with the idea of 'exiling' parts. This was introduced to help people understand the role of their parts and how we often behave towards them. It gives us a way of understanding what happens when we are embarrassed or ashamed of a part. Or if we are told that we must not be like this. We 'exile' the part, banish it from our presence. The other parts then stand 'on guard', making sure this part does not return.

Well, I understand the idea, but covering our parts with other parts always made more sense to me as this way of thinking accepts that the original part is still with us, just hidden. Let me make clear what I mean by covering. Using a typical example from my work an angry part may be 'covering' a sad part. What this means in practice is that when any situation threatens to 'trigger' the sad part, the angry part 'covers' the sad part with anger. So, no one ever sees the sad part and, even worse for your chance of making progress, you forget that the sad part exists and think your problem is anger.

This idea of a new part being constructed to cover the earlier part makes sense to me for several distinct reasons, I'll go through them one at a time.

1. *It helps me to understand the sequence of parts construction.* How old they were when covered etc. Obviously the earlier the part the smaller the doll. This offers a visual clue as the ages of the various parts.
2. *It helps me to see how they are trying their best to help me by the covering process.* The new part is constructed when the trauma, shame or embarrassment of the earlier part needs to be hidden. The new part completely covers the one before it with new strategies and behaviour.
3. *It helps me to work with them in the right order.* The size and positioning of the dolls gives a helpful visual aid and helps me to explain why we need to work with the earlier part first.
4. *It helps me to explain the process with a visual aid.* Using the dolls put together, taking them apart as we work, or just having them all apart from each other. All this helps to show the client a fitting example of how our brain is working to protect us.

But the most important reason is rather more profound, especially to a Christian perspective. You see our parts are trying to do the absolute best they can for us. In doing so they are mirroring what Christ did for us. You may have heard of the idea that we are 'covered by the blood of the Lamb'. This is Jesus' blood and is the only way we know of getting into heaven, because when God looks at us, He sees Jesus. By allowing his blood to be shed He paid a great price for us. Your parts are also sacrificial, they are covering what they think of as your sinful nature as best they can. Of course, it does not work well because any new parts are still part of the sinful nature themselves! It can motivate us to want to build a better relationship with our parts once we understand their sacrifice. I have seen people go straight from hating their part to feeling the love and compassion of Christ for the same part, just by understanding this.

'I' is a complex statement

When we say 'I' in western culture it is shorthand and makes social life, rules and legislation possible. When working with clients and listening to their experiences I found it made more sense to think of our 'self' in a more complex way. I want you to adopt this complexity as a new way of working with your inner self. You will have experienced many times the way your imagination works separately from your conscious mind. Those times are amazing when your imagination delivers a solution, or an answer. Without this creativity we would not have maths, poetry, architecture or anything creative.

I'm a Christian, so why am I still...

If you have ever said "I'm in two minds about that", or, "I don't know what came over me" then you realise that you have always known about this complexity. What about the time a football player had a much better second half and we say, "he gave himself a good talking to at half time". Even though we acknowledge this idea in the way we speak, the 'medical model' has prevented us from really accepting it and working with it. The Church has joined in and demonised it whilst medicine has pathologized it. To use the Biblical model, you first need to accept that it is perfectly normal to have different beliefs, opinions and attitudes within you.

Before you can understand how these 'parts' work, we need to look at the environment in which they operate. How best to think of your 'front room', the place where you live and where all these decisions are made. It is a very special place in the Bible called the upper room.

The upper room

The Upper Room, also known as the Cenacle, is in the southern part of the Old City of Jerusalem on Mount Zion. It's where the Last Supper took place. It's where the apostles stayed when they were in Jerusalem. It's where Jesus washed his disciples' feet (John 13:1–20). It is where the concept of a loving friendship with Jesus was introduced, which we know from John 17, sometimes known as the "high priestly prayer". It is the place where the disciples gathered in fear after the death of Jesus, and it's the place where they prayed, with Mary, for the coming of the Holy Spirit (John 20:19–23).

The Cenacle is considered the site where many other events described in the New Testament took place, such as:

- preparation for the celebration of Jesus's final Passover meal Luke 22:13
- the washing of his disciples' feet John 13:4-11
- certain resurrection appearances of Jesus Mark 16:14 - Luke 24:33 - John 20:19
- the gathering of the disciples after the Ascension of Jesus Acts 1:13
- the election of Saint Matthias as apostle Acts 1:15
- the descent of the Holy Spirit upon the disciples on the day of Pentecost. Acts 2:1-4

This room is also the room where Jesus appeared, both before and after the resurrection. It was here that Jesus allowed Thomas to see and touch his wounds. It is where the Lord breathed on them the Holy Spirit "on the evening of that first day of the week" (John 20:19). It is in this same room where tongues of fire appeared to the disciples on Pentecost and "they were all filled with the Holy Spirit" (Acts 2:4). It is from this room that the apostles went forth with boldness sharing the Good News. It is in this room where the disciples became one in spirit and commitment to the Lord Jesus.

But it is also the room where they gathered in fear and locked themselves in.

> On the evening of that day, the first day of the week, the doors being locked where the disciples were for fear of the Jews, Jesus came and stood among them and said to them, "Peace be with you."
>
> John 20:19

Jesus saw the absolute terror that was upon them and repeated his blessing

> Jesus said to them again, "Peace be with you. As the Father has sent me, even so I am sending you."
>
> John 20:21

Notice that even after the Lord had appeared to them and offered his peace to them. Even after they had been raised from the dead and had entered through locked doors, they still had the doors locked eight days later when he returned to them

> EIGHT DAYS LATER, HIS DISCIPLES WERE INSIDE AGAIN, AND THOMAS WAS WITH THEM. ALTHOUGH THE DOORS WERE LOCKED, JESUS CAME AND STOOD AMONG THEM AND SAID, "PEACE BE WITH YOU."
>
> JOHN 20:26

At this time he breathed on them and asked them to receive the holy spirit. This was after Thomas, who had not been present at the first meeting, had been given the opportunity to place his hands in the wounds.

You have an upper room of your own. It is your frontal lobes. Your consciousness. This is the filter through which everything must pass and where your understanding develops. This is the place where you will work with your inner disciples and help them to come into harmony with you. Like Jesus' disciples, your parts will accept you as their leader once you accept that it is your role to be their leader as part of your commitment to them. Remember that the same spirit breathed on the disciples in the upper room lives in you. When they see the same level of commitment and love from you that the Disciples saw in Jesus, they will follow your commands in the same way the Disciples followed Jesus' commands.

When I work with my private clients, I talk about their 'upper room' almost from the start. I describe it as 'the room where everything happens. The room where you live. When you consider everything I have said in this book so far about your growth, it is inside your upper room that you have assessed and decided on everything. Think of your upper room as the place where everything is imagined and decided. It's the place where you spend time with the parts that will become your disciples.

When you experienced traumas or unhealthy behaviours in others, your brain learned that certain areas of this 'room' were 'no-go' areas. Just like the disciples not showing their fear to Jesus, your brain learned not to show you these areas. The main difficulty with this is that you were not able to 'make sense' or to 'process' or 'clean up' these parts of your life. This led to even more difficulties as you go through life with these 'blind spots'. Growth starts when you understand that you are the one that is going to change this. That you are responsible, willing and able.

It is quite common in my practice for people to tell me of troublesome dreams of past times at a stage when they are doing well in their growth and expect better experiences. A typical example of this would be someone getting over alcohol dependency dreaming of themselves being horribly drunk. They are often very disturbed by these dreams, thinking that this means that it will happen. However, I explain that this is because they have now 'given permission' to their brain to make sense of what has been a 'blind spot' and that this is a good sign. As your brain makes sense of this part of your life it becomes a memory and becomes part of your past.

To work with yourself effectively and to make your room fit for the Holy spirit to live in, we must give ourselves permission to clean and organise it. This starts by bringing your peace to this room the same way that Jesus did. It may surprise you to think of your mind this way, but this approach will produce a clear and healthy mind. The psychological advantage of a healthy mind is a massive reduction in anxiety and intense emotions. You may be shocked to find how much energy you have been using to keep yourself from seeing some of this mess.

> THEREFORE, CONFESS YOUR SINS TO EACH OTHER AND PRAY FOR EACH OTHER SO THAT YOU MAY BE HEALED. THE PRAYER OF A RIGHTEOUS PERSON IS POWERFUL AND EFFECTIVE.
>
> JAMES 5:16

The most important thing is that you are cleaning the room so that the Lord's voice can be heard much more clearly. You can begin this work immediately by accepting your state. Before you begin the work of inner discipling, show your intention by cleaning up the room you have invited Jesus to live in!

Go to God and your accountability or prayer partners now with your resentment, your fears and your dishonesty. It may be easier to be accountable in your life now that you see a real purpose for doing so. See it as the first step in your life of inner discipling. Remember that if you do not do this you will simply be another house divided against itself.

The house divided against itself

> FOR THE FLESH DESIRES WHAT IS CONTRARY TO THE SPIRIT, AND THE SPIRIT WHAT IS CONTRARY TO THE FLESH. THEY ARE IN CONFLICT WITH EACH OTHER, SO THAT YOU ARE NOT TO DO WHATEVER YOU WANT.
>
> GALATIANS 5:17

To fully understand and work with the Biblical principles used by this approach we must first tackle the issue of metaphor in the Bible. I say this not because metaphor is a bad thing, or because people do not understand it. Rather I say it because of one particular problem I see a lot in Church teaching. This is the way we understand the **metaphor of fighting**.

When you heard preaching on the parable of the sower I'm sure none of you thought of yourselves as dirt! When Jesus says he is the way, he is not saying he is made of tarmacadam! When you heard references to these parables, you naturally understood that these were metaphors. But there is something about the idea of fighting a battle that encourages people to forget that this is a metaphor just like the rest! I think it's because the medical model has us so busy believing that we need to get rid of 'wrong things' in our lives. This medical idea resonates so well with scriptures about battles that we mistake the **metaphor for the real thing**.

In Galatians 5, verse 17 quoted above, the more modern the version of the Bible you read, the more the language of fighting is used. Where the older versions use a more measured approach, saying that the spirit and the flesh are 'contrary' to one another, or 'in opposition'. Modern versions tend to be more material saying that "there is a constant battle raging between them". This is important when considering your thoughts on this approach because modern Churches tend to teach from more 'modern' Bible translations.

The point here is that as long as you are fighting this battle you are a 'house divided against itself' (Matt12:22) and you miss the growth and learning you need to make progress. More on this later along with other problems that fighting with yourself can bring. For now, I'm asking you to consider the idea that scripture does not ask us to fight with ourselves, only that there are parts of us in opposition with our true selves.

There was a battle in heaven and Satan and his followers were ejected. There was a battle for your soul and Jesus won that one for you. I want to encourage you that the battle is the Lord's (2 Chron 20:15). I could go on. But let me move away from persuading you against this idea and move towards the example we will be using almost exclusively. In this book the main example you will be following will be the way Jesus managed and taught the Disciples.

Jesus's relationship with the Disciples

> AFTER JESUS HAD FINISHED INSTRUCTING HIS TWELVE DISCIPLES, HE WENT ON FROM THERE TO TEACH AND PREACH IN THE TOWNS OF GALILEE.
>
> MATTHEW 11:1

I want you to try now to imagine what Jesus saw when he looked at the disciples. When God looks at us, He sees our evil nature in a way that we cannot even imagine. The Bible says that he prayed all night and then came down from the mountain and chose the twelve from among the main group. Now I want you to consider something. Remembering that Jesus is perfectly aware of their sinful nature and called them evil to their face (Matthew 7:11), what did he do with them?

These are questions I ask every Christian I work with. Did Jesus fight with the disciples? No! Was what Jesus taught in opposition to the way the disciples were living? YES! Please don't think that the time of Jesus' birth was random. It was prophesised to the exact day! One likely reason why the Lord came down to earth at a time when Israel was occupied by the Romans was to show us that fighting was **not the way**. Even when they wanted and expected that their King would stand up against the Romans and defeat them, he did not. He told the disciples to pray for their enemies!

Even though he had a much better understanding of their sinfulness than they did, he did not fight with them but loved them and taught them. Slowly but surely creating harmony between them. Helping them trust him as their Lord and Saviour took years of commitment. You have begun to do the same thing within yourself and now it's time to use this improved relationship to face the challenges of the outside world.

From an inconsistent 'self' to a set of consistent 'selves'

> Then the devil left him,
> and angels came and attended him.
>
> Matthew 4:11

I want you to now picture a spectrum. This spectrum has at one end every normal human being and includes basic ideas of escapism as well as 'being in two minds'. Any time we have wanted to eat a big chocolate bar or other food we know is not good for us or wanted to watch a film or read a novel when we know we should be working we are forced to conclude that there is more than one opinion going on in us! We are seeing the complexity of the human condition. This is perfectly normal and includes the idea of escapism or 'exits' as a way of coping with stress. Including watching telly or reading a novel after a day's work to 'wind down'. At this end of the spectrum, it is perfectly normal.

The other end of the spectrum includes PTSD and dissociative disorder, the profoundly serious form of trauma and 'triggering'. This extreme reaction may need some counselling or Pastoral support. Somewhere in the middle is where most addicts, dependencies and unwanted behavioural patterns are found and where you are likely to be. If you are experiencing more serious symptoms of trauma, you should consider finding a specialist trauma therapist as part of your plan. If you have been diagnosed by a psychiatrist with a mental condition you should take advice before continuing with this approach.

The Construction and role of our parts.

> THE MIND GOVERNED BY THE FLESH IS HOSTILE TO GOD;
> IT DOES NOT SUBMIT TO GOD'S LAW, NOR CAN IT DO SO.
> ROMANS 8:7

So, to understand these new findings and how we are going to use them we first need to understand what is meant by our 'parts'. How they are constructed, how they function and why they sometimes 'take over'. As I said earlier this 'taking over' is part of your natural defences and is a good thing. It has been designed into you and is extremely useful when it works as it should. If there is a crisis, your brain will get you out of it a lot faster and better than your mind will!

The abilities of your mind tend to get in the way during an emergency. Things like ethics, morals, aesthetics and appetite will not help you if the building is on fire. The part of your brain that reacts to threat is an extremely basic part. Biblically it is understood as the flesh, scientifically called the prehistoric or reptilian brain. It has no moral sense. It has no sense of time (to your brain it's always 'now'). It does not share your concern for others. It only cares about one thing and one thing only. Your survival!

All well and good so far. Your brain, which is lightning fast, steps in to protect you when there is a threat to your life. When there is no threat, your brain allows you (your mind) to run things and make decisions. So, what's the problem? I hear you ask. The problem starts when life (your experience) teaches you that something is a threat when it isn't. Because this part of your brain does not exist in time it often reacts to something that was a threat to you when you were much younger. Something that would not be a threat to you now as an adult. That is what can make these brain interventions harder to spot because your brain is reacting to something and taking over when there is no need.

On these occasions your mind would be much better at dealing with what is in front of you, but your brain is insisting on taking over. Apply this back to the disciples. They had to choose to follow Christ. Jesus did not force them to obey him, they could have turned away from him any time they chose, and some of them did. Your brain is in a similar position. Remember that your mind cannot shut down your brain, but your brain can shut down your mind!

Before you start to use these ideas, I want to say some more about the way your brain processes the information it receives. All day long your brain is receiving information from your senses and your life experiences. I use the word information carefully since the idea of what is 'real' and what is 'imagined' is more the way your mind would construct things, not your brain. Your brain receives information and acts upon it. Think of this part of your brain like a computer. As I type on my laptop the computer receives the information from the keys. The question of how 'real' the information is does not arise within the computer. This is why we can have real feelings when watching a film even though (in our minds) we know that it's just actors reading scripts with lights and cameras. Your brain receives the information from the film and acts upon it without making much of a distinction between what is 'real' and what is 'imagined'.

The front room and the back room

The front room that we have talked about is your mind, your conscious self. The back room is your brain. Whereas your conscious self in the front room has a timeline the brain in the back room does not. When we use blended language to describe our parts or inner disciples we are combining or 'blending' what we need to separate or 'unblend'. Included in the front room is your development and change through time. You are not the same person you were when you were twelve years old. You have matured, learned and grown. Physically, mentally and spiritually. You have changed your opinions on things, just look at the change when you came to believe! However, the notion of change is very different when we consider the back room.

Rather than a room where change takes place through the passing of time, think of the back room as a room with shelves on the wall. When things (events) are placed on those shelves they stay there until someone moves them. If you returned to that room in a hundred years, those things would still be on the shelf! In other words, something your brain holds to be true, for instance that certain things are dangerous and must be avoided, will remain true for your brain until you change it. Just like the Disciples, their world would have remained the same forever if Jesus had not come and produced the evidence for change. Just like the Disciples, your brain works on evidence. Your practice is to produce evidence that our brain can believe in.

So remember, any talk of timelines must relate to your core self (the front room) and not the 'parts' you have (the back room).

The three choices of the brain

If I asked you what your brain does with the information you give it, what would you say? Something about the role of memory, possibly. But memory is only one of three options. Mostly what your brain does with this new information is to discard it. Let's take these three options one at a time.

Option One - the bin

By far the most common choice as you pass back a ton of unimportant information through your sense is for your brain to say, "we don't need that" and in the bin it goes. This is why you can't remember everything like what shirt you wore last Tuesday, or what you had for breakfast. Result - this is probably gone forever.

Option Two - the memory

The second most used option is to pass the information into memory. This information considered to be more valuable and so the brain decides to keep it. Your memory is what you use to process and 'story' your life. As things happen, we make meaning and decide what a thing is. Then we 'pass' it into memory. It becomes part of our past, our story. This is called 'recall memory' and becomes something we can refer to later, like getting a book from a shelf. Result - You are not living with an awareness of this stuff, but you can access it at a later date.

Option Three - Take a snapshot

By far the least used of the three options is to keep it rather than throw it away or pass it into the memory. Whenever we are threatened in a way that seems to be serious the brain does not throw it in the bin, nor does it allow it into the memory but 'stores' the event in a specialist part of the brain known as the amygdala. Imagine this snapshot being 'pinned' to the wall in your back room. Result - not part of your memory but pinned to the 'wall' of your brain for quick access. This means that it is sometimes not something you can remember (recall) which makes it very difficult to understand and resolve.

Effectively taking a 'snapshot' of the event, your brain then acts in a comparable way to the customs officers at the airport or Harbour in passport control. As the arrivals pass through, the officers compare the faces they see with the faces on their screen. If they see a face that matches one on their screen, that is when they call in the support. Just like those Officers, your brain stays on alert looking out for anything that looks like that snapshot on the wall. Remember that the depth of the trauma is not measured by the nature of the event but rather the effect it had on you. Something that would not bother one will traumatise another.

Now this work your brain does, can be particularly useful of course. At the time it happened it can help you stay alive in a life-threatening situation. But it is about 'survival' and will never be about anything else. Any strategies or behaviours you developed to cope with these threats will also be about survival. It is important to remember that there is no growth in any of this. It is just your brain's way of keeping you alive.

A survival strategy is considered successful when you are still breathing at the end of the day. It has no other aims. Again, no problem if we are dealing with a genuine threat to your life. The problem starts when we enter adult life and do not swap these strategies for what I call 'flourishing' or growth strategies. Remember, the place where your brain has pinned these experiences to the wall has no timeline. The neuroscientists put it this way they say, ***"your amygdala cannot tell the time"***. In other words, if you do not remove or replace this snapshot, it will stay there forever. Notice how this matches the Biblical view that your spirit is concerned with eternity, whereas your flesh is all about now!

When I start to work with my clients this way, they often say things like "oh that was ages ago. I have not thought about it for years". The problem is that the trauma is stored in the back room which has no sense of time. Even though you have not thought about these things for years, you are carrying them around with you every day. With your brain ready to 'take over' any time there is anything that is reminiscent of the snapshot. I often describe it this way. Imagine yourself in a restaurant with friends. They are laughing and joking, eating and enjoying themselves in a relaxed atmosphere. You are sitting there in a suit of armour with a machine gun!

Now always remember, the threat does not need to be a real threat to you today. This was maybe threatening to you as a baby or child. It is not necessarily a threat to your adult self. Take separation for example. If your Mother left you on your own a lot when you needed to connect with her, your brain will react to this snapshot every time someone threatens to leave you, or if it seems that someone else is getting their affection instead of you or even if you get the sense that they might be thinking of leaving! This would have been a threat to your life as a baby, but this is not a threat to your adult life!

It's not the feelings but the proportion!

One of the best ways to identify your 'parts' behaviour is to match the reaction with the circumstances. Always look out for your reactions that are way too big for what has just happened. Don't be tempted to think of some feelings as 'good' and some as 'bad'. This is a step back into the medical model. All feelings are appropriate, given the right circumstances. Some of the most infuriating people we meet in Church are those that think like this and so always appear to be deliriously happy! This is not Christlike and does not replicate his behaviour as any brief reading of scripture will confirm.

When you are triggered, the feelings you will experience will be hugely out of proportion to the event. If this happens to you, remember that you will often be experiencing the feelings of a much younger self. Always assume that this is a part, not Christ living in you. You will have been triggered by the threat and your brain will be running the show, not your mind. Here are three things I want you to learn about your 'parts';

1. They are constructed through trauma.
2. They are triggered by threats.
3. They are always trying to help.

Let's now compare this with the disciples' position prior to their discipleship.

The disciples were traumatised

Prior to the Lord beginning to disciple them the disciples were traumatised by being occupied by the Roman Empire. I recently visited France and took a tour of the landing sites of the British and their allies during the second world war. The photographs of French people staring out of their doors and windows at German troops marching down French streets with tanks and guns gave me a totally different view of the War. As England was never occupied during this time, we did not learn what it was to be occupied. Occupation is traumatising! Just like the disciples, you have had some experiences of threat in your life that are stored in your brain and are being acted upon.

The disciples were threatened

They were all finding ways to cope with the occupation. From Simon the zealot who wanted to fight them, all the way to Levi the Tax collector who wanted to work with them and everything in between. The disciples were looking to their own ideas as to how to deal with the threat of occupation. This is exactly what your 'parts' are doing. They, like the disciples, are offering you the best solution and strategies that they (in the flesh) can come up with. It's so important that you grasp this idea that your brain is not against you. It's offering you the best it has. Unless you get this idea, you will be constantly drawn back into a **fight with yourself.**

The disciples were attempting to overcome

> NOW IF I DO WHAT I DO NOT WANT TO DO, IT IS NO LONGER I WHO DO IT, BUT IT IS SIN LIVING IN ME THAT DOES IT.
>
> ROMANS 7:20

How do you feel when you read the Bible and see what the disciples got wrong? Do you feel sorry for them? Do you sometimes hate them for deserting or denying the Lord? Do you look down on them for locking themselves away when they were afraid? Are you disappointed when they go back to their life of fishing after the Lord had been crucified? Or do you sympathise and think of the errors they made as the inevitable consequences of reliance on the flesh? In the practice section you will learn about the 'observer position'. This is vital to your growth and progress, and it always comes from a compassionate place!

When you start to work with this Biblical approach, it is so important that you shift away from inner conflict. Just like the disciples, your parts are trying to make a good thing happen. Your brain is not trying to trip you up or ruin your life. Always remember that the reactions you experience come from this 'snapshot of trauma'. They are the best your brain has to offer.

I have experienced tremendous progress with clients using this understanding and arrived at it from years of experience, particularly when clients talked about their experiences of when things got 'out of proportion' (something counsellors are looking for all the time as it means that the unconscious is involved). These are always described either as uncontrollable rage, unmanageable emotions or terrible decisions.

In the more traditional approach to this issue of the flesh we will often hear phrases like "they are in the flesh" when describing traumatised attitudes, reactions etc. Notice how this conforms to the medical model in the way it sees the person as one very inconsistent thing. To me, that's like blaming the car when a reckless driver steals the car of an incredibly careful owner and smashes it up. That's not the fault of the car!

When we place addiction and dependence difficulties in the context of 'parts' that need discipling, we understand ourselves in a more logical way. It offers us a clear understanding of why we sometimes feel that we are going crazy because of our extreme reactions. We start to understand the way we can go from having such a commitment to our recovery one minute and not caring about it the next! It offers us a simpler way of understanding the way we are motivated and driven by our unseen 'parts'. It gave me a way of working effectively with people and helping them to grow spiritually in their recovery.

So, it may seem clearer now that different 'parts' of you are 'running the show' at various times. Understanding this difference as behaviour happening in separate rooms. One (upper) room in which your conscious mind lives, and another (back room) where your brain operates. In this way the Bible offers us a way of thinking which will be really helpful when we start the work of cleaning it up! Reactions are from the back room; responses are from the front or upper room. Once you have grasped this important difference you are ready to begin your practice.

CHAPTER EIGHT

The practice

So, you now understand yourself a lot better. You have a clear picture of how you are more complex than you thought, and a more measured and useful idea of the true nature of sin. Those apparently 'crazy' behaviours and thoughts now make more sense. But how do you work with this new understanding of your 'self'? If you are going to use this approach effectively, it's not just a matter of understanding yourself from this perspective. You need to develop methods to face every challenge. Methods that go along with the approach. You need to learn to work with and not against yourself in your practice. Learning to work with your inner disciples is where all the progress takes place.

So, I want to first describe the process of transforming your language from 'blended' to 'unblended', which will help you understand when your brain is intervening and in which way. Secondly, I want to give you a better understanding of how to take the 'observer position'. It is from this position that leadership and course correction take place. I have found that the best place to start your practice is with your everyday language. Particularly the way you talk about yourself.

From blended to unblended language

One of the most important aspects of the 'medical model' is the way it produces 'blended' language. Blended language is defined as any form of speaking or writing that 'blends' everything that you are into one thing such as 'I'. In this way everything you do or say is attributed to 'you' even though the behaviour and attitudes may completely contradict how you feel or the values you hold. Let me give you a few examples of how to spot blended language.

Example One
Blended statement
I used to be really organised and calm but now I panic over the smallest things.
Unblended translation
I am really organised and calm but there is a very panicky part of me that is triggered by the smallest things.

Example Two
Blended statement
I used to get so angry when he said things like that but these days it doesn't bother me so much
Unblended translation
My angry part is triggered by things he says but these days that part trusts me to handle it.

Notice in example one that the timeline is present (I used to be - but now). This timeline is the way we usually make sense of any changes or inconsistency in our speech attitude or behaviour. The unblended translation removes the timeline (I am - but there is) which separates the two states (rooms) and attributes them to 'parts' and 'self'. So, in unblended language there is usually no change over time. Rather it allows for different parts being in the 'driving seat'. This eventually relates to how much you are 'trusted' by your brain.

In the second example the timeline is also present (I used to - but these days) but the unblended translation includes the way we can convince our parts to trust us (that part trusts me). This is the main way that 'parts' change, which is to learn to trust our core self. Just as the Disciples learned to trust the Lord.

Developing an unblended language is one of the first changes we can make. It is when we try to practice this new skill that we often realise just how much the traditional (medical) model has dominated our thinking.

When you say 'I' you are generally referring to a single entity, you! Of course, this makes sense from the perspective of pragmatics, shorthand and common sense. We are delineated by our physical self, we are 'individuals', responsible for our decisions. This approach is not an attempt to avoid responsibility, we are culpable and accountable for everything we do. It is unavoidable and reasonable that when we do something we are going to be held responsible for our actions unless we are diminished in a legal sense.

Clients often tell me of decisions they made and things they have done. These things seemed crazy to them as they sit with me and talking calmly about them later.

At times like these I often ask, "we both support different football teams don't we"? "That doesn't seem crazy to you does it"? Of course it doesn't. Because there are two people and two opinions. As soon as we separate out the parts that have different opinions, it all makes sense. It's only when we try to squeeze all our conflicted opinions into a single self that we can feel crazy.

> FOR I KNOW THAT NOTHING GOOD DWELLS IN ME, THAT IS, IN MY FLESH. FOR I HAVE THE DESIRE TO DO WHAT IS RIGHT, BUT NOT THE ABILITY TO CARRY IT OUT.
>
> ROMANS 7:18

Ask yourself this, is Jesus inconsistent? Was he changeable and moody? Christ in you is just as consistent as when he walked the earth, and once you accept this then it becomes obvious that when you behave in ways that you do not like or want, other parts are involved. These other parts are just as consistent as your core self, but from a fleshly perspective. They have different strategies and beliefs about what will help. With practice you will learn all about these parts, how it feels when they take over, what they are certain about, what they are triggered by and when they were formed. But you can only do this well when you stop fighting them!

To practice the method that follows, and to overcome what has stood in the way of your development, you also need to understand and work with the 'observer' position. It is from this position that you can begin to separate yourself (Christ mindedness) from the other parts (disciples) you have. It is from the observer position that you can start to empathise with your parts and the way they are trying to help you. It is from this position that you can teach them and ask them to trust you. It is from this position that they will recognise you as their leader. So, what do I mean by the observer position?

The observer position

> BUT HE SAID TO ME, "MY GRACE IS SUFFICIENT FOR YOU, FOR MY POWER IS MADE PERFECT IN WEAKNESS." THEREFORE I WILL BOAST ALL THE MORE GLADLY ABOUT MY WEAKNESSES, SO THAT CHRIST'S POWER MAY REST ON ME.
>
> 2 CORINTHIANS 12:9

How do you decide what you think about something? How are you viewing and thinking about your own behaviour? One of the main keys to this whole approach is what I call the 'observer position'. It is only from this position that you can begin to work with the parts that are protecting you. We have already looked at one of the best examples of this in the Bible, which is the prodigal in Luke 15 and verse 17. When the younger son 'turns again to himself' he is taking the observer position. He is looking at himself from a position that does not come from his feelings or difficulties. Rather it is a position that sees these things from a higher perspective. It is Gods view.

The observer position is your Christ mindedness working in you. When you asked him into your life, he promised he would come in and be with you (Revelation 3:20). He then lives in the upper room of your mind and helps you understand and correct your behaviour through His truth.

I want you to think about the last time you acted out of proportion. It could be you got angry over some small thing. It could be the last time you were really frightened over something that held no real threat to you. It could be the last time you overreacted to loneliness by watching porn or overreacted to anxiety by taking drugs or drinking. Have you spent too much time at work as a way of avoiding people? As long as you believe these things to be 'you', the only response will be the usual stuff of shame, self-loathing, with maybe some denial and fighting etc. But once you know that it is a 'part' of you that acts autonomously and has different opinions from your adult self, you can use these times to make progress by taking the observer position!

So, the next time you are 'out of proportion' in your feelings, thoughts or attitude, try to avoid judging yourself and observe what is happening. A quick point here about feelings. Most people reading this will believe that it is the type of feelings they are having that is the main problem. If you are often feeling angry or depressed, frightened or lonely you may think of this as your problem. It makes sense then to develop strategies that help you avoid these feelings, such as taking drugs or drinking alcohol, gambling or watching porn. All of which dull or remove feelings. But I want you to know that **the feeling is never the issue**. It is **the proportion of the feeling when compared to the circumstance** that is the issue.

If your reaction is in proportion to the circumstance, then it is the result of harmony in you. When you react in a way that is out of proportion you can be certain that you are in a triggered state and that a part (your brain) has taken over.

This is inner conflict or the loss of inner harmony. In other words, there is no such thing as a 'bad feeling'. Jesus was angry (Matthew 21:13). Jesus was sad (John 11:35) and Jesus was frustrated (Matthew 17:17) He was anxious (Matthew 26:39). So, remember, it's not the feelings but always the proportion that's the issue.

Confirming the Observing position

> HE TENDS HIS FLOCK LIKE A SHEPHERD: HE GATHERS THE LAMBS
> IN HIS ARMS AND CARRIES THEM CLOSE TO HIS HEART;
> HE GENTLY LEADS THOSE THAT HAVE YOUNG.
>
> ISAIAH 40:11

When you try to observe your parts behaviour and beliefs, you first need to think about who's doing the observing! Please do not shy away from the challenge of this tricky idea! If you are going to make the most of this approach, you must be able to differentiate between your parts acting out on their beliefs, and your Christ minded self which observes this.

Develop the sense of standing back and observing yourself. Describe your feelings, thoughts, attitudes and actions in the **third person**. Coming from God your Christ mindedness is untainted by the world. No matter what your experience has been, no matter how abused you have been, no matter how cruelly the world has treated you. Your resources as supplied by God stand separate from the world. Remember, it's peace beyond all understanding!

It is only from this Christ minded position that you should begin to disciple your flesh. If you try to do this without an understanding of who is doing the observing, you will often fall into the trap of one part observing another! Think of this as like the Disciples, when they were trying to guide each other such as in Mark 9 and verse 33, where the Lord asks them what they were arguing about. Well, they were arguing about what parts always argue about, namely, which of them is the greatest! Your parts will always judge and fight with each other, because they are flesh.

So how do you confirm the observer position? The way to check this is to see if, when you observe yourself, you feel judgemental, ashamed or otherwise negative about the part. If you do, stop! This means that you have not achieved the observer position. Even though observing is taking place, it is not you but another part of you that is observing the first part! Remember, your parts do not always like each other. This may seem complicated at first, but it is just part of your complexity. The main thing to notice is compassion. If you hate your part and wish it were dead, this is not Christ like and is not the way to good discipleship. Step back again and watch the second part watching the first part. Now check if you have compassion for them both. Only when you feel compassion for what you are seeing can you say you have achieved the observer position.

There are many examples of this in the Bible. When the Disciples were arguing among themselves about who was the greatest, Jesus saw multiple positions taken by multiple people, but he had compassion for all. The

Disciples certainly would not have liked the idea that Matthew joined the group, since he was a tax collector and therefore the lowest of the low in their eyes. There were several times when they were arguing amongst themselves such as Matthew 20:24, John 6:61 and John 12:4 where Judas complained about the cost of the perfume. The practice is always to step back once again. Notice any part with strong feelings, watch out for any judgemental part watching the first part. Ask yourself again, do I now feel pure calm and confident clarity? Repeat this process until you can answer yes to these questions. Only then will you have Jesus' view, filled with compassion for your lost sheep (Matt 9:36).

You can also include any time you feel in two minds about something. If you find one part arguing against another, or feeling ashamed of the other, always try to step back and take the observer position. Continually checking that your feelings about these parts are connected and compassionate. As you continue in this way to reposition yourself you will notice that your thoughts become calm and clear. That you feel courageous and confident and that you are curious to know more. It is only from this place that inner discipling can start, because it is only then that the authentic self (Christ mindedness 1 Cor 2:16) is doing the observing. You will have the mind of Christ.

It's also worth remembering that parts can also imitate things like calmness, courage and confidence. It may be a way of being at work or with other people. It may be a skill that your part learned through years of practice. Remember Peter, imitating courage when he said, "this shall never happen to you" Matt 16:22. This was not courage, it came from his flesh, which is why Jesus rebuked him.

The way to discern if this is a part or not is to ask yourself how you feel, not how you look or appear. If you are honest with yourself, you will recognise those times when you **look** calm but **feel** anything but! If you see something that looks like imitation or mimicking, step back again. With a little practice you will learn to step back into the observer position and restore your resources of calmness, clarity, creativity, confidence, curiosity and courage, compassion and connectedness.

Back to the Prodigal!

There are many examples of this transformation brought about by the observer position in the Bible, but the prodigal son is one of the best. We all know about and what an amazing story it is. You will remember that the son has spent everything he has and is sitting with the pigs feeling deeply sorry for himself. I want you to revisit this moment now from this 'observer' perspective. In verse 17 of chapter 15 in most modern versions it says 'When he came to his senses'. In more traditional versions it says, 'When he came to himself'. In the Wycliffe version it says, 'and he turned again to himself'. Most people will have read the modern versions and missed a vital point here. Which self is turning to which self?

Notice that the self that does the turning is perfectly calm. Knows exactly what to do, what to say, where to go. Notice also that the circumstances seem like a shock to this calm self. Note the incredulity" How many of my father's hired servants have food to spare, and here I am starving to death"! Note the surprise. It's almost as if this part of him does not know what has been going on. Note also that every decision made from this point on is the right one. Everything he says, everything he does, every attitude he displays, they are all perfect. Whereas before verse 17 every decision he made was the wrong one.

This is how it is with every 'rock bottom' with every 'moment of truth'. The authentic self has been absent. The 'part' or parts have been running the show. How long do you think it took him to spend his inheritance? It could have been several years! But the idea that there was a part of him (greedy and resentful) that had completely taken over becomes the **most rational explanation**. Once the authentic self returns, the right decision is made instantly. No matter how bad the situation is. Isn't it an encouraging idea that you have just the same resources as this prodigal son Jesus was talking about!

> ALL THINGS WORK TOGETHER FOR GOOD
> TO THOSE THAT BELIEVE
>
> (ROMANS 8:28)

It always becomes clear, at some point, that we are employing an unhealthy strategy. At some stage it must become obvious that it's not working! Thank goodness that it does! It always seems to me that this is the one consistency in any unhealthy strategy, any of Satan's tactics. When someone with addictive vulnerability takes drugs for the first time it seems like the answer to everything, but eventually, the disaster of this strategy is exposed.

I'm sure that, for a while, the prodigal thought he had everything life could offer. Enough money to pursue every fleshly desire, lots of friends paying him compliments and celebrating with him. It was only when the money ran out and a natural disaster struck that the unhealthy nature of this strategy was exposed. And it was this that led to his return! Learning to see God in our unhealthy attitudes and behaviour is a massive step forwards in our ability to grow. Not because He wants us to fail. It is the suffering that is produced by our fleshly solutions that causes us to turn back to him and submit to His ways.

The first time I got drunk it was like magic. I felt no fear or anxiety. I could say anything to anyone and felt confident. Fifteen years later I was a total mess. The point is that if that strategy had not made that mess, then my 'adult self' would not have returned to sort things out. I remember that moment when I said something similar to the prodigal. The moment everything changed. I was suddenly open minded to solutions. I was able to face discomfort and to see the sense of looking at my failings as a way forwards. Up to that point I could not have done that because, like the prodigal, the part of me that was running the show was threatened by the idea of flaws or being mistaken.

Re-triggering your core self

So how do you manage yourself once you have named a triggered state? The question I want you to ask will always be prefaced with the words "I wonder". "I wonder what state is this"? "I wonder which part is this"? When you start a question with 'I wonder' you evoke curiosity which is one of the core states! This often has an immediate effect of re-triggering the adult or 'core self'. If you ask simply "what state am I in"? Your part can answer "I'm angry of course"! But parts are never curious, they are always certain. Only your core self will be interested in a question that starts with 'I wonder'.

I talked earlier about shifting from a reaction to a response as quickly as you can. This is because a response is from the 'front room' and would be a way of re-triggering the core self. But there is more you can do. Of course, I am assuming that you are not completely overwhelmed by your 'state' which would mean there was no core self 'present' to do anything! This is what happens with extreme PTSD and should be dealt with through counselling specific to the issue.

Most of you will not experience anything like this feeling of being 'overwhelmed' but will usually feel some sense of the true self being present. This presence may be experienced as questions such as "why am I doing this"? And "What am I saying"? It can feel like you are watching yourself without any control over what you are doing. I am going to offer you four simple steps to re-triggering the core or real self. Think of these steps as ways you would stand, talk, breathe and look if you had perfect faith! As you get to know your parts better and better and learn to disciple them you will learn about how they stand and talk, what they think and believe, even how they breathe and what sort of facial expression they have.

Here are four simple techniques to 're-trigger the adult'.

1. **Body language** - Check your posture. It was said that Jesus resolutely set out for Jerusalem (set his face like flint) Luke 9:51. Every 'part' will have some sort of postural style. So, sit up or stand up straight. Remember the last time you felt really confident about something. Stand or sit like that. When soldiers are on parade, they do not tell them to put their shoulders back, their chest out and their chin up randomly, it's for a purpose. When you improve your posture, you will improve your core presence.

2. **Breathing** - Your 'parts' are likely to affect your breathing as adrenaline or some other chemical change takes place. Again, slow down and deepen your breathing to come into line with your calm and clear core self. Again, it's no accident that lots of approaches will say "just take a breath now" or "take four deep breaths". From a medical point of view this would be to calm you down, but from this perspective we would say that you are accessing your calm self.

3. **Facial expression** - Almost every 'part' of you will bring their own facial expression. Angry parts will

screw your face up. Depressed parts will let your face droop. Look in the mirror when this happens and relax your face where there is any tension and allow yourself to regain your calm, clear, core expression. Again, use scripture and any experience of past confidence to help you with this.

4. **Tone of voice** - It almost goes without saying that each part will have their own tone when it comes to your voice. If there is a fearful part taking over, your voice pitch may drop and become quieter. You may start to talk slower. If there is an angry part present, then the voice is likely to be raised in volume and be at a higher pitch with a faster pace. You may also notice that certain parts use certain words, this is another way to identify them. Remember Peter's accent being one way he was recognised in Matthew 26:73. Pay attention and observe your tone. Consciously return to your calm vocabulary, pitch and volume.

CHAPTER NINE

Inner Discipleship - towards harmony and growth

So how do we bring all this together? I want you to take the idea and importance of 'inner harmony' from John 17, discussed earlier. Then add the idea of 'discipleship' as Jesus taught it and lived it out. Where does this take you? How do these things fit together in a way that helps you to grow spiritually? I have introduced you to the idea of 'inner discipleship'. If these ideas get you feeling a little wobbly, remember the 'evidence based' ideas from neuroscience that our parts are natural and not pathological.

The men who became disciples were just living natural lives. Trying to make a living and get on in the world. Their ideas of how best to manage were formed by the circumstances they were in. Remember that they were traumatised and oppressed! They were taught a world view that forever condemned them to feel bad about themselves. Always under the power of the Pharisees and the occupation of the Romans. When Jesus said "I forgive you" it threw them into a dispute with the world that condemned them, but it created harmony within them!

You are caught in the same trap that the disciples were in but possibly for varied reasons. Their trap was the weight of God's law and their sinful nature. Today it may be more about the medical model and how it creates and constructs our thinking. Either way recovery and growth become possible when we are released from the trap and live in forgiveness and harmony. The trap of judgement brings inner conflict and self-loathing. Freedom through forgiveness offers you an opportunity for better relationships, particularly with yourself.

When you hate that part of you that sins and gets you to do things that are unhealthy or wrong you enter a battle with yourself that you are probably going to lose. There is little chance that your mind is going to beat your brain! This is just the sort of trap that Satan wants you in! An everlasting battle that you can't win. What a distraction! Staying in that trap guarantees that you will not be doing the work of the Kingdom effectively. When Jesus told us of the good news, he released us from this trap and yet so many of us return to it!

In my work with addicted people, I always start at this point. I make sure that my clients understand that to recover they must develop a better relationship with themselves. To avoid this horrible trap, they must stop hating themselves for the thing that they do. Paul helps us to understand this in his first letter to the Corinthians.

> For, "Who has known the mind of the Lord so as to instruct him?" But we have the mind of Christ.
> 1 Corinthians 2:16

It can be difficult to shift from a massive cultural idea such as the medical model and the judgement and the self-loathing that comes with it. You may find that the biggest difficulty you have is facing a fear that your issues will run amok if you stop fighting them with everything you have but I have found this is rarely the case. If you have the desire to work with your parts, reassuring them that you (your Christ mindedness) are present, willing and able to handle whatever they feel they need to protect you from. That you are more than able to manage this challenge. Like the Disciples with Christ, they will learn to trust you and stop insisting on this way of protecting you.

This is just what Jesus did. He showed them that he was with them, fully present and able to deal with any and all difficulties that they faced. Many times saying, "fear not". Offering them new and better ways of managing themselves in difficult circumstances. All the way through the Old and New Testament God reminds us that we do not need to fear. Nowhere better than Psalm 23

> EVEN THOUGH I WALK THROUGH THE
> VALLEY OF THE SHADOW OF DEATH,
> I WILL FEAR NO EVIL, FOR YOU ARE WITH ME;
> YOUR ROD AND YOUR STAFF, THEY COMFORT ME.
>
> PSALM 23:4

When Jesus was left with the woman caught in the act of adultery (John 8:11) it is important to recognise that he condemns the sin but loves the sinner. "Go now and leave your life of sin".

So, it's time now to make the brave decision to develop a new relationship with your parts. Just as God did when he sent his son. Instead of punishing yourself for not following the rules, it's time to work with your parts lovingly, appreciating what they are trying to do instead of blaming them for what they produce. You can only do this from the perspective of knowing that they are always trying to make a good thing happen.

Christ in you

> FOR THE WORD OF GOD IS ALIVE AND ACTIVE. SHARPER THAN ANY DOUBLE-EDGED SWORD, IT PENETRATES EVEN TO DIVIDING SOUL AND SPIRIT, JOINTS AND MARROW; IT JUDGES THE THOUGHTS AND ATTITUDES OF THE HEART.
> HEBREWS 4:12

Remember, the aim is to get the brain to trust the mind. To get the flesh to trust the spirit. As it already does in most circumstances. This trust is developed firstly by the recognition that a message of 'follow me' has been delivered. This recognition is supported by the way your messages line up with the truth. When Jesus said "follow me" the 'Disciples to be' recognised the truth of what was happening, and who he was. Your parts will recognise Jesus in you.

Developing a better relationship with your parts

> I DO NOT UNDERSTAND WHAT I DO. FOR WHAT I WANT
> TO DO I DO NOT DO, BUT WHAT I HATE I DO.
>
> ROMANS 7:15

When you think about your attitude towards your parts, what do you see? Have you generally hated those parts of you? Have you been trying to hide them? Do you tend to deny them? This attitude often leads to other parts protecting you in more serious ways. Have you been ashamed of them and prayed for them to be removed? I want to encourage you to follow Jesus' example in getting to know your parts.

As you read what Paul writes about 'himself' he starts to talk about his 'parts'. Speaking very rationally he shows his wisdom by saying that if he does something he does not want to do then it is not him that does it! This is so sensible! Why on earth would you do something you do not want to do! But I am sure that you have read this, as well as receiving teaching and preaching on the subject. The problem comes in the way we understand what he says next.

He says that rather than him doing this, it is sin that 'lives in him' that does it. It is likely that we think of this as something to be removed as evil and this is often supported by the teaching we receive from the Church. But as I have already argued, if you take the simple idea of sin as something to hate (which we should) without the understanding that your 'sinful nature' is both inevitable and an attempt to help you (even though it is misguided and naive), you simply construct a conflicted self that cannot produce the inner harmony that Jesus is praying for in John 17. When you take the perspective that your sinful nature is doing the best it can but needs educating and leading, you have a picture that starts to line up with the way Jesus saw the disciples.

Why is Judas here?

But wait! I hear you say. I'm with you so far, but what about Judas? Jesus didn't say he needed correcting. He said he was a devil! (John 6:70). So, first things first. Let's remember that Jesus chose him. Choosing Judas was not a mistake. He was supposed to be there to be who he was and to fulfil scripture. So how should we understand this? You have read in my personal story how God through his holy spirit 'blew the madness out of me' during the few seconds of my healing. Jesus chose Judas so he could be removed.

I completely accept that it is part of the model that there are things in us that need removing. In fact I am blown away that God has included it in the model! I am sure that you as a Christian have been prayed over many times. I am sure that you have prayed yourself and fasted over your issues. You have probably been prayed over by Elders or preachers that have visited your town. So, your faith tells you that what God needed to remove he has removed.

If the removing part has been done, please do not become one of those people that returns to Conferences and gatherings time after time, year after year expecting God to do something that, in fact, he has already done. Please don't waste time praying for God to do things you can do for yourself.

The kind of distinction I am asking you to make is found in Matthew 12:31 where Jesus says that 'every kind of sin and slander can be forgiven' and that sins against 'the son of man' will be forgiven. But sins against the holy spirit will not be forgiven. It is this idea sometimes called a *'wilful rejection of grace'* that is unpardonable and must be removed from us. This type of sin is contrasted with the way that *sin and slander* can be forgiven.

Just like Jesus with the disciples, you should not remove every part of you that is not pure, or does not understand, or is acting in a naive way. Just like Jesus, work with these parts. Disciple them. Love them and guide them. Help them become who they are supposed to be. Let's now look at the kind of things your parts have probably been suggesting to you.

Why is Levi here?

> Once again Jesus went out beside the lake. A large crowd came to him, and he began to teach them. 14 As he walked along, he saw Levi son of Alphaeus sitting at the tax collector's booth. "Follow me," Jesus told him, and Levi got up and followed him.
>
> Mark 2:13-14

Like Judas, you may wonder why Levi was included in the disciples. To the other disciples he was a sinner, shunned by his fellow Jews as a tax collector he would not have been automatically accepted as one of them. As we read in the second chapter of Mark, Jesus reminds the Jewish religious leaders that the 'exiles' are the ones who need help the most.

Exiles

Levi represents a particular form of 'part' or disciple known in therapy as 'exiles'. They are the parts of us we are ashamed of and often hate. Attempting to get rid of and disown them, we often pretend as if they do not exist. It is these parts that we need to disciple the most. Acting as if they are not part of us simply develops the fragmented self which will always be in conflict and which will never 'stand' (Mark 3:25).

So, Levi does belong in the disciples. But like the others must be transformed into a disciple from someone who is going his own way and applying his own solutions to the issues he finds. As part of his discipleship, Levi becomes Matthew and writes the Gospel of Matthew. He abandons his own ideas (Luke 5:28) and joins a unified team of disciples. Creating more inner harmony for the group.

Levi would not have been acceptable as 'discipling material' by the other disciples. However, Jesus calls him, and he instantly follows (Mark 2:14). Later Jesus visits Levi's house and dines with him. He also takes the disciples (Mark 2:15) and this offers us a perfect example of how we will manage our 'exiled parts'. Notice that when the Pharisees ask why it is that Jesus is eating with sinners and tax collectors (exiles), it is not the disciples who answer the question but Jesus himself. They would not have known the answer as they would not have chosen to do this 'sinful' act. Jesus says that he has not come to call the righteous, but sinners (Mark 2:17). Jesus is asking the disciples to put harmony above sinfulness. To accept Levi, the exiled one, not because he was righteous but because he was chosen.

Remember that for the disciples (other parts) this is all about training. They had been trained to think of tax collectors as people to be despised. They would have been trained in all manner of ritualised practices as part of their teaching that would be designed to keep sin away. But this was not the only time that Jesus challenged their teaching about 'exiles'

The disciples were shocked when Jesus asked them to walk through Samaria instead of going round. This is one of the biggest cases of 'exiling'. The Jews hated the Samaritans because they were Jews that had married outside the race. The Disciples would have never gone there and would have protected Jesus from the Samaritans, but it is no accident that Jesus uses the Samaritans in several examples of 'goodness'.

Exiling as covering

Earlier in the book I mentioned parts 'covering' other parts as a way of protecting you. When the Disciples saw that Levi was to become one of them, they wanted to exile him. Think of this as 'covering' him. In other words, making him invisible. What parts have you exiled (covered)? What parts of you have you become ashamed of? What parts of you are you pretending do not exist anymore? What parts of you have you been fighting with? Like Jesus in Mark 2 and verse 15, you can begin to disciple these parts by welcoming them back into your life and winning their trust. Watch them abandon their own understanding and be guided by your Christ mindedness.

Understanding the way your disciples protect you

As you develop better relationships with your parts through greater understanding of the way your life's experiences have trained them, you will begin to recognise the conditions that trigger them into action. Once you have a good grasp of this common sense will lead you to the conclusion that it is the situation you find yourself in that causes the 'parts' to react. This is not true! It seems obvious because these are the conditions that trigger the reaction, but this is very misleading! What they are really protecting you from is the possibility of **the exiled part returning** (the covered part being seen again). Think in terms of the disciples and everything they had been taught from childhood about exiles and what they had to do to prevent them (and their sinfulness) from returning. Let me give you an example to make this clearer.

Adams covering

Adam is a professional and is struggling with cocaine and gambling. He enters treatment and we discuss the conditions that cause him to want to use drugs or gamble. Themes emerge around anxiety at the thought of disappointing people or being caught doing something wrong. We explore the roots of this, and he remembers being naughty as a child and being caught. He remembers these occasions as 'nothing bad happened' in terms of punishment. But the effect on his brain is much more serious. Even though his common sense tells him that he is being protected from being caught, I invite him to explore at a deeper level. What would happen if these anxious parts did not protect him? Then the exiled (covered) part would show up. We train our brain that this must not happen! So, the therapy helped Adam to understand that his exiled part was one that did not follow the rules and wanted to be getting something for nothing. His other parts (such as the drug tal]king part) were doing their absolute best to not allow this selfish part to be seen by anyone.

Martha's covering

Martha was a professional person in a caring role. She entered treatment because she could not stop drinking. When we explored the circumstances that triggered the drinking thoughts, we discovered various parts including an angry part and a part that was constantly anxious about being taken advantage of. Exploring the themes in the circumstances that surrounded the drinking there was always something about the possibility of being seen as hopeless or useless! This is the 'exiled' or 'covered' part.

The history or source of this part is in Martha's parenting or peer led experience. One way or another she was convinced that being 'hopeless or useless' would get her rejected. This leads to the 'exiling' of this part. The main effect of covering is that the brain is then 'wired' to be on the lookout for any circumstances that may lead to someone seeing this part of us. Other parts are developed such as Marthas 'busy and capable' part. This should help you to understand the real nature of 'triggering', the triggered parts are taking over to protect us from the deeper, covered part being seen!

Once Martha understood the nature of the triggering, she could be supported in creating inner harmony by appreciating the way her parts were protecting her. This therapeutic work always includes getting the parts to trust her, but this is only effective if you are willing to allow the covered part to be seen. So, her practice was to find something that she was hopeless at! This turned out to be playing guitar. Martha had bought a guitar years ago and really struggled with it, eventually giving it up. I asked her to get it out again, practice up to the level where she struggled, and then welcome the hopeless part. This practice also included reminding or retraining the other parts to accept the hopeless part. The fringe benefit of all this was that she stopped drinking!

As you learn more about the way life has trained you to 'cover' certain parts of yourself, you will get more insight into your reactions. It will become increasingly clear to you why some of your parts have been covered and that you have trained other parts to keep it that way. You will become much more familiar with the feelings, and attitudes that go with them. Along with the behaviours that they produce.

The disciples recognising and following Jesus.

> WHEN SIMON PETER SAW THIS, HE FELL AT JESUS' KNEES AND SAID, "GO AWAY FROM ME, LORD; I AM A SINFUL MAN!"
>
> LUKE 5:8

Everyone who has met with the Lord will recognise him and never forget their encounter. One of the main things I try to get across in the early part of my work with new clients is that their parts will recognise the adult in them once they meet him or her. I often tell the story of the youngster who arrives home to find no adult there. They feel that they have to do something for their younger sister, such as make a meal or clean up. When the adult finally arrives home to find the mess that has been made the youngster feels nothing but relief because there is an adult here to take over, and the adult appreciates the effort without condemning the child for making a mess! I want you to learn to appreciate the efforts of your parts as they recognise the adult in you.

There are many examples of this in the scriptures. When Jesus said to Andrew and Simon "follow me and I will make you fishers of men" in Matthew 4:18, He was using the fact that they were fishermen and connecting this with the more important idea of winning people to the truth. He was asking them to make that shift from what they thought was their life to what the Lord had planned for their life. From who they thought they were to who they really were! Whereas when He walked past two of John's disciples, it was maybe the fact that they were already disciples that motivated them to follow the Lord (John 1:37) after they heard John say who Jesus was. In John 1:43 Jesus reveals himself to Nathaniel by knowing what had happened to him even though they had never met. This is yet another way that we can meet the Lord.

What you are going to see next are things you will have all seen before. There are many good studies on the disciples and their shortcomings, as well as their successes and strong points. The difference here is that you will be separating yourself (your Christ mindedness) from them. Whereas studies and messages you have heard up to now have asked you how much you, as a person, are like them. How much you share their weaknesses. Which encourages a combative approach. This approach is asking you to watch them from the observer position as separate from yourself and to commit to teaching them to trust you and allowing you to handle things from now on.

Jesus did this in Mark 6:46-47 when he observed the disciples from a high mountain whilst they were struggling to row against a strong wind. He saw their fear and confusion. He also calmed them when they thought he was a ghost! You may also find your parts not understanding you when you first communicate with them. There is so much for you to learn about your parts as you develop this approach. And there is so much for them to learn about you! For now, let's look at what you are likely to find when you start to observe your parts.

CHAPTER TEN

Recognising your parts

> I NO LONGER CALL YOU SERVANTS, BECAUSE A SERVANT DOES NOT KNOW HIS MASTER'S BUSINESS. INSTEAD, I HAVE CALLED YOU FRIENDS, FOR EVERYTHING THAT I LEARNED FROM MY FATHER I HAVE MADE KNOWN TO YOU.
>
> JOHN 15:15

In Mark 4:13 Jesus chooses the twelve of his disciples that will become the apostles. He does this after spending the night in prayer. This is a huge decision because it's only possible for you, me, and any other person to be a Christian because of these twelve and what they did. In your recovery you have it a lot easier. Your inner 'disciples' or parts are already built into you by design. But you may struggle at first to recognise them. This is because of the power of the 'medical model' and the way we are all influenced by it. Remember, you have been told that you are a single entity, confused and inconsistent. And that you need to change and be cured or fixed. The Biblical approach says that you are a multifaceted entity, clear and consistent, and you don't need a cure!

Depending on what your struggle is, you will recognise various parts here. You may not recognise all of them. For now, just take on board the idea that each of the disciples' attitudes were things that represented the best they had and were designed to help but were usually **naive, radical and immediate**.

All your parts essentially derivatives of the four categories of flock, flight, fight and freeze. This is their designated role, but they have been recruited by your experiences into unnatural roles. When they start to trust you, they will return to the role they were designed to have. I want you to make your own study of this, but for now let's look at some of the ways the disciples were and how Jesus responded to their behaviour and attitudes. Learning about their issues and the way Jesus taught them and helped them to develop is extremely instructional.

I find there are broadly three ways to convince 'parts' to 'step back' and return control to our 'core self'. They are

1. **Authoritative** - In the form of a strong but not aggressive command. *In Matthew 26:52 "Put your sword back into its place. For all who take the sword will perish by the sword".*
2. **Affirming** - In the form of a request couched in an approving message and loving tone - In the form of total appreciation in the request. *In John 1:47* - When Jesus saw Nathanael approaching, he said of him, "Here truly is an Israelite in whom there is no deceit."
3. **Loving** - *In Matthew 16:17 And Jesus answered him, "Blessed are you, Simon Bar-Jonah! For flesh and blood has not revealed this to you, but my Father who is in heaven.*

I want to encourage you to do your own study of the times when this teaching and correcting takes place but here are a few that I have learned from. Remember, all your parts are derivatives of the main four - flock fight flight and freeze. So, I'll start with them and then add a few other examples that you may identify with.

Flocking

> BUT HE DENIED IT BEFORE THEM ALL.
> "I DON'T KNOW WHAT YOU'RE TALKING ABOUT," HE SAID.
> MATTHEW 26:70

Flocking is one of the most common of your brain's reactions to threat and we see examples of it in herd animals that confuse predators by mingling together. Since predator's hunt by singling out a target, there is safety in merging.

The herd mentality

Did you ever find yourself denying something that would make you stand out from the crowd? Did you ever react to the crowd's hostility and do something just to blend in? Peter did it three times in one night. Twice because he had been seen with Jesus and once because of his accent. In his desperation he cursed and swore at the crowd, insisting that he did not know Jesus.

One of the most common ways of flocking is seen on the school playground. You may remember strong feelings of needing to have the same clothes as your peers. It can feel like a matter of life and death for youngsters to have the 'right' jeans on or the right trainers.

Jesus' response was to cook him breakfast and to confirm the love he had for him. John 21:15. Another instructive lesson on how to manage the relationship with our parts. Jesus had already told Peter that he would deny him three times.

Fighting

Reacting to threats aggressively is one of the most common reactions. If you react this way, you may well be hating yourself for the things you have said and done. This reaction of the brain to threat is well known. Did you ever say, "I don't know what got into me". Or "I just saw red and lost control". This is Peter in you. He once attacked a guard and cut off his ear because of anger (John 18:10). What was Jesus' reaction? We see it in verse eleven.

> BUT JESUS SAID TO PETER, "PUT YOUR SWORD BACK INTO ITS SHEATH. SHALL I NOT DRINK FROM THE CUP OF SUFFERING THE FATHER HAS GIVEN ME?"

First comes the authority in the form of a command, "put your sword back into its sheath". This example is clearly an authoritative intervention, with Jesus taking the position of Master and quickly restoring control of the team. The second half of the statement is affirming, letting Peter know that by taking over at this point he is getting in the way of what needs to happen.

We should not shy away from this authoritative voice when it is needed. In Matthew 16:20 Jesus uses this voice again to all the disciples.

> THEN HE STERNLY WARNED THE DISCIPLES NOT TO TELL ANYONE THAT HE WAS THE MESSIAH

In Mark 3:17 Jesus names James and John 'Boanerges' meaning the 'sons of thunder'. Again, this is relating to angry reactions and flying off the handle.

Grandiosity

Did you ever make a grandiose statement about your faith and commitment that you later regretted? Did you sound like Peter who once rebuked the Lord and said, "this will never happen to you" (Matt 16:22). This is another common reaction of your parts to threat.

Notice how the reaction of Peter here is naive and leads to Jesus saying *"you do not have in mind the concerns of God, but merely human concerns"* which perfectly describes the difference between the adult and the parts. Between the spirit and the flesh, between your mind and your brain, Christ in you.

Greed

> THOSE WHO WANT TO GET RICH FALL INTO TEMPTATION AND A TRAP AND INTO MANY FOOLISH AND HARMFUL DESIRES THAT PLUNGE PEOPLE INTO RUIN AND DESTRUCTION.
> 1 TIMOTHY 6:9

Did you ever act greedily or selfishly? Thinking only of yourself? Of course you have. Did you look like Judas in Mark 14:10 who, along with others, had lied about wanting to give the money to the poor by selling the perfume. When the truth is, he just wanted the money for himself. And seeing that perfume worth 'a year's wages' had been 'wasted' by anointing the Lord with it, he then went to the Pharisees. Offering to betray the Lord for money.

Ambition

Have you ever thought about what you might gain from being a Christian? Does it remind you of James and John? In Mark 10:35 they asked, "Grant us to sit, one at your right hand and the other at the left hand, in your glory".

Flighting

Did you ever act out of fear or run away from your responsibility? Fuelled by adrenaline you have been managed by a quite common reaction to threat. Did you look like Peter in Luke 22:57 when he said "Woman, I do not know him". Or was it more like the disciples when

Jesus asked them to feed the crowd? saying "where are we to get enough bread in such a desolate place to feed such a crowd"? Mark 8:4

Scripture was followed when the sheep were scattered (Matt 26:31), and the Lord knew very well that it would be so. You should never expect mature or wise behaviour from your parts. Until they accept you as their Lord and Master, they will act to protect you any way they can. It is so important that you proceed knowing this so that you will not hate yourself or the part when you disappoint yourself.

Flight parts are not always as obvious as they might sound. When Peter said "I'm going fishing" in John 21 and verse three, you may not have recognised this as a flight part but simply thought that he is returning to what he knows. This past lifestyle is his security and the rest follow him, but they catch nothing. Flight parts protect you by suggesting things that give you an 'exit' from your situation. Peter didn't know how to stay in the position to which he had been called, so his 'exit' was to return to what he was doing before he was called. Whenever you have a thought suggesting returning to old addictive or dependent ways, this is a flight part.

Doubt

Did you ever struggle with trusting the word of God? In John 20:24-31 Thomas said that he would not believe until it was proved to him, contradicting the level of faith that we are asked for. Your doubt part is another variation of a flight part. Notice that Thomas could escape the responsibilities and the pressures on his life if he demanded proof.

Fear

You may have already realised by now that fear is another flight part. As long as something is frightening you can avoid the tough choices and actions. Did your parts ever boast about their commitment to the Lord, making a big noise about your courage? Was it like Peter in John 13:37 when he said, "I will lay down my life for you". Like him, did you find yourself unable to follow through with this commitment?

Notice that in all these examples there is no hatred of the behaviour or attitude. There is correction in different forms, but it is always respectful of the motivation and desire to help.

Later I will take you through the exercise where you can begin the work of discipling your inner parts. As you get better at this you will learn to recognise the distinctive characteristics of the disciples (parts) you have. Whether it's a 'Peter' or a 'John', A 'Simon' or a 'Matthew'. You will learn how to accept your parts, appreciate them and teach them to trust you.

Freezing

> BUT WHEN HE SAW THE WIND, HE WAS AFRAID, AND BEGINNING TO SINK HE CRIED OUT, "LORD, SAVE ME."
>
> MATTHEW 14:30

We have all read about the time when Peter walked on water. Having asked Jesus to call him he actually got out of the boat and found himself doing something miraculous! Then comes that word 'but'. Did you ever find yourself called out, singled out? No longer in the protection of the group. Doing something extraordinary. Or you may not have noticed what the threat was. The triggering may seem to come from nowhere. The effect of freezing was there for all to see, he started to sink! He lost the power to do what he was doing.

The most typical effect of a freezing part is to stop speaking. Therapists usually refer to this as 'shutting down'. Freezing moments do not always come from miraculous moments! Often, they are a part protecting you from a more obvious threat. As well as feeling unable to speak, freezing parts can prevent you from getting out of bed in the morning, applying for jobs or college, asking for a date. Often a flight part will protect you in a frozen position by suggesting a return to drink or some other familiar unthreatening behaviour.

Shame

> AND WHEN THE TEN HEARD IT, THEY BEGAN TO BE
> INDIGNANT AT JAMES AND JOHN.
>
> MARK 10:41

Shame has something of a special place in this order. We all know how debilitating shame can be but when you think of it as a part of you it is worth developing your understanding of the way this part is often a 'polarised' part, performing a type of balancing out position of other parts.

Did you ever become indignant at yourself (or worse) after you have behaved in an unhealthy way? The other disciples did after they heard a request from James and John to "Let one of us sit at your right hand and the other at your left in your glory" in Mark 10:37. This will often happen with your parts, one or more parts taking an opposing position. Apparently 'balancing out' or 'polarising' as it is known. This often shows up as shame or indignation around your weakness. It is particularly important that you recognise this indignation as parts behaviour. Do not mistake it for your core self. Your Christ mindedness would not feel that way.

This is an example of parts reacting to parts, which is again quite common. Whenever you have acted in this grandiose way ask yourself this, "how do I feel about this part"? If you are feeling ashamed, then you can be sure that this is not your core self but more likely another part. Remember that parts are certain, they believe they know what is right and what is wrong. They also disagree strongly with each other often which is what polarisation is about.

Take the time to locate your Christ mindedness which is shown by a calm clear compassionate state. Speak to each part lovingly from this position. Watch how Jesus creates harmony and restores relationships here by reminding them that they should take any motivation towards being grandiose or lording it over others and translate it to serving all. This is affirmative teaching. Here we see the wonderful, appreciative truth the Lord brings.

Did you ever feel ashamed of who you were? Did it remind you of Simon when he said to Jesus "Go away from me, Lord; I am a sinful man! But Jesus said, "Don't be afraid; from now on you will fish for people". Jesus is showing us how to work with a shameful part. He is saying "from now on" which is to say think more about what is going to happen rather than what has happened already. Talk to your parts this way. Encourage them by what you are heading towards and how you will all be working together.

Becoming your own primary caregiver

You alone handle the state of your upper room. If it gets untidy, you are the only one who will clean it. Do not expect God to do it! If you are allowing your younger and less wise parts to run the show in there, it is you and only you that is going to do something about that. If we have invited the Lord to live there, we should make it as fit a place for him as we possibly can. But not by fighting! We will achieve this by accepting personal responsibility for the cleanliness of the place.

If you have avoided this responsibility for years by 'exiting' your upper room with drugs or drink or some other behavioural escape, or by being angry or afraid, then the idea of taking responsibility will be alien to you. Firstly because of how effective 'exiting' seemed to be and secondly because no one else can see what a mess there is up there!

Over time this develops a dependency pattern of avoiding processing our feelings. This leads to a belief that we are not supposed to feel anything difficult or uncomfortable. This practice inevitably leads, over time, to greater dependency and addiction. The answer is to take responsibility.

Jesus took responsibility for what he was given to do. Look for a time in the Gospels where the Lord allowed the Disciples to use their own fleshly ideas to achieve Kingdom aims, trust me, you won't find it. Can you now accept that this also applies to you and your own way forwards? Allowing your parts to run your life is like having very young relatives with you and, when things get difficult, asking them to deal with it. This is never going to turn out well.

As a Christian you have the Lord Jesus living in you through the Holy spirit. He will act through your core self in any situation you find yourself in. He will lead you towards the truth of your circumstance and the correct way to deal with it. Look at what he was able to do through the Disciples! There is nothing that He cannot handle through you. There is nothing you cannot handle with his help! But winning the confidence of your parts so that they trust 'you' to handle these situations is a big part of that help. Just as the Lord won the confidence of the disciples so that they accepted him and his way of doing things.

CHAPTER ELEVEN

My own journey of inner discipling

I have been working with my own parts for several years. It's important to remember that my experience of working with addiction and dependence stretches over several decades. This means that my understanding has developed massively over these years. It may be useful to offer you a brief history of my development. Once I have described how my understanding has developed, I will include a short section on how I am living with my parts these days.

My first experience of reverse addiction triggering that I can remember was when my dad brought home a stray kitten he had found. We were left alone with this kitten and my two younger sisters were desperate to hold it. Of course, it was terrified and hid under the chest of drawers. I can still feel the anxiety that gripped me at the time as I felt a huge sense of responsibility towards this kitten. This responsibility was way larger than it should have been. Somehow, I had been trained to see others welfare as my job.

My first experience of addiction triggering was when I first got drunk. The level of relief I felt was amazing. I only knew how much anxiety and pressure I had when it went away! Needless to say, this child being drunk was embarrassing, at least it would have been if I had cared. But that was the point, I didn't care! Like all addicts, my entry into addiction was an escape from reverse addiction. It was the best idea that my flesh (parts, brain) could come up with. It worked or seemed to work for several years but eventually was revealed as the disastrous strategy it always was.

The first time I was introduced to anything that resembled a 'parts' approach, was many years after I had recovered. I had been sober fifteen years and had begun working in rehabs. Although there was lots of talk of 'parts' in various forms, none of the work was informed by neuroscience as it is today. The main difference was that none of these methods unblended and separated the disciple (part) from the (Christ minded) authentic self.

The fact that I and many others managed to recover without any understanding of parts, reminds me that people recover in many ways. This helps me to remain open minded when working with people.

King Baby

This approach appeared in a book (King Baby Syndrome) written by Tom Cunningham that owed a lot to Freuds 1914 paper 'On narcissism'. When I began working in Rehabs, it was commonly used to explain narcissistic behaviour and attitudes in the clients. There was often talk in group sessions about the enormously powerful idea that the Baby within the addict is also a king. However, the 'King baby' was understood as an immature motivation of the self. Once the addict is educated to notice this 'presence', it becomes just another way of hating yourself.

As part of the medical model, it was often used to critique client's behaviour and thinking, especially immature or selfish motives. Rather than a therapeutic tool, it was considered more as a way that someone was or behaved that needed to be dominated or beaten. Although some considered it as a permanent issue for the 'addictive personality'.

'My addict'

The idea of 'my addict' appeared later, as I remember it, and involved a more substantial method behind it. Unlike the King Baby, this 'part' was identified as separate from the self and something that could 'think for itself'. This was progress as it opened more discussion and therapeutic possibilities, but the idea was still strongly linked with the medical model. Not so much because it did not separate the part from the self, but because it constructed the 'part' as a medical problem, an illness.

This meant that the 'inner addict' was always constructed as something to be removed. Especially the problematic idea of 'spiritual sickness', which can be found in the Big Book of Alcoholics Anonymous. This meant that it became just another thing to hate, to fight and to defeat. Leading to more conflict and self-loathing. I was never fully comfortable with this idea as our spirit is from God (Genesis 2) and cannot be sick. Gods spirit is pure and perfect.

Voices of influence

When I started my training as a systemic therapist, the idea of what a human being is began to be expanded in my understanding. Following this training we would often ask about the clients 'voices of influence'. But these were considered as 'introjects', influencing voices from care givers, parents, friends and teachers etc. Essentially this was a throwback to Freud and so did not usefully separate the self or take the complexity and ability of the brain into account. When we worked with this idea, it was mainly to help the client see the influence of others on their lives. The main therapeutic motive was to support the client through 'psychoeducation', which would help them to understand where these 'voices' came from, and support in 're-authoring' their lives. This meant that this systemic idea remained firmly in the medical model.

Inner discipling

It wasn't until I was introduced to the work of Dr Schwartz that I really stepped into the possibilities of using the complexity of what a human being is. Because Dr Schwartz is a systemic therapist and received the same training as myself, it really helped me to 'get' the idea behind his work. He was essentially saying that all the methods and techniques that we were using with families could also be used 'internally'. He found that the ideas were just as effective when thought of as the clients 'inner family'. The assumption was that each person effectively lived with an 'inner family' and could develop relationships with them.

The most critical point about this was that it was **not based on the medical model**. In other words, it was not presented as part of a sickness or that this was something that came from outside of yourself. This meant that each inner family member 'meant well' and was not part of an illness or condition. Although this was a giant step forward for me, it wasn't until God showed me that this was the way people were created and just as His word describes.

Following this, I started to read the Bible very differently, especially the New Testament. This was the beginning of inner discipling. My work with others, both as a psychotherapist and Pastoral worker has become so much more effective since gaining this understanding.

My parts

As well as what you have just read, you will probably conclude in what follows that my parts are quite typical to a lot of my clients. I hold this to be an advantage for me in my work with others. With that in mind, I want to first show you how understanding of these things usually develops in client work. Everyone is unique and individual so don't worry if your parts don't turn out to be the same as mine or anyone else's. Here is a list of the stages I see often in my client work. I have numbered them in the order they often develop.

1. **Having parts is not an illness** – Moving from a medical model to a Biblical model is the first and largest hurdle clients get over as they courageously begin to explore themselves beyond the teaching of their culture. It offers us the possibility of working with our parts rather than hating them.

2. **My parts are trying to help me** – the next logical step once you stop thinking of yourself as broken, sick or ill, is to understand your brain (flesh, parts, disciples) is trying to help you! Learning that your brain is part of your sinful nature is a huge step. Like Jesus, you can become a friend of sinners, starting with yourself!

3. **My part can learn to trust me** – the next step is to see the possibility that our brain (flesh, parts, disciples) will allow us to run our lives once we are trusted. Remember that your brain is already trusting you to run most of your life (it's likely to be doing it now as you read this). Just like the disciples learned to trust the Lord, learning to produce evidence to support your claim leads to spending more time in your Christ minded state.

4. **I have more than one part** – most of us will already be aware of one main part. Even though medical science has discouraged us from mentioning it

by pathologising the idea of 'voices'. Once we acknowledge the first 'part', we can learn how other parts are present, how they are 'triggered', and how they fit together.

5. **My parts are sequential** – as our understanding develops, we get to know our parts better. This includes the idea that, not only are they at different ages and levels of maturity, but also that they were constructed in sequence. One part leading to another.

6. **Each part protects you from the prior part** – the next step in the process is often an understanding of the way one part was constructed as a way of protecting ourselves from the previous part. I call this 'covering' and give examples of this in my story that follows.

7. **All parts are welcome** – Once we have a grasp of the true meaning of our sinful nature, we can develop a more complete attitude of loving acceptance towards all our parts. This is the final step in going from a conflicted self to developing a harmonised self.

Learning about my own parts

My main part has me acting out in egotistical ways, often encouraging me to claim more than I am capable of. In this respect he is a lot like Peter.

I had wrestled with him for years and years, sometimes trying to hide him and sometimes pleased with him, but it was only when I developed this method that I could understand him and develop a better relationship with him. Since this part was not a result of illness, I could stop fighting it. This helped me to look beyond the typical conflict, shame and embarrassment of thinking of myself as ill, and begin to work with the part 'Peter' was protecting me from.

The part Peter was covering was a much younger part that had been ignored and was incredibly sad. Frightened that he would be forgotten or rejected (always the main concern for your brain), he would want to shrink and isolate. The egotistical part is constructed to hide the sad part (which your brain has been trained to hide from everyone). This part then 'covers' the sad part by overreaching and fantasising about success and receiving admiration etc. From then on, whenever circumstances threatened to trigger the little sad part, the egotistical part covered him with pride and boasting.

My drinking and drug taking part was constructed around the age of fifteen when the egotistical part was getting me into too much trouble. There were many times at school when I could see that my egotistical part was annoying people and getting me a bad reputation. Self-preservation probably played a part in constructing my drug taking and drinking part by anaesthetising the boasting part.

This drinking 'addict' part is also egotistical, but the anaesthetising effect of the drugs meant that I didn't care so much. The egotistical part always believed that I would prove these claims to be true eventually anyway. Sometimes, in an inebriated state, the ego, the drinker and the sad part would all be present and the chaos that ensued became more and more tragic.

Typically, of people who become addicted, the problems that arise through the actions of the addicted part lead to a huge set of separate problems that take years to develop, and even more years to face. Once sober, learning to separate these two sets of problems is fundamental for anyone wanting to develop a quality recovery.

When I work with people these days the progress and transformation come much faster because of this understanding that parts are sequential and always cover the prior part. Instead of fighting the larger, outer part, we ask this part to trust us to work with the smaller inner part. I will now describe the idea of inner discipling on a more general level. This will help you to apply this approach to yourself as we move into the practise section.

CHAPTER TWELVE

Discipling your parts

> IF YOU THEN, THOUGH YOU ARE EVIL, KNOW HOW TO GIVE GOOD GIFTS TO YOUR CHILDREN, HOW MUCH MORE WILL YOUR FATHER IN HEAVEN GIVE THE HOLY SPIRIT TO THOSE WHO ASK HIM!"
>
> LUKE 11:13 NIV

Well, I want to say well done for getting here! You have listened to a lot of ideas that may be new to you. You have maybe been challenged by some or all of what you have heard. You may have struggled to accept some things that have gone against decades of teaching and efforts on your part. The fact that you have stuck with it so far is an achievement. All you have learned provides the context for your practice and for doing the work of recovery and growth.

In this section of the book, you will be using lots of examples from the Bible where Jesus worked with the Disciples. This means that you can also make your own study of the scriptures. This will give you a coherent approach to developing your relationship with yourself as you follow the Lord's example. But before we get to any of that, let's start by using an exercise I want you to use many times. The more you use it, the more you will understand your parts and the more they will understand who you are.

Think of this practice initially as a meditation exercise as much as anything else. So don't rush anything. I want you to think of situations where you acted out of control. It doesn't have to be a complete loss of control, maybe just what you would call 'out of proportion' behaviour. But where there has been some sense of not being fully in control of yourself. So, this could include times when you get angry, times where you have become frightened. Times where you have become greedy or times when you have become overly defensive. And of course, times when you have 'exited' through any addictive or dependent behaviour. There will often be a pattern or theme you can learn about here because your parts have learned (from your behaviour) to watch out for certain 'triggering' events.

A lot of you will already have these times in mind and will know exactly what I want you to focus on, but don't worry if it is not immediately obvious to you. This 'blankness' is sometimes one of the ways your parts will protect you. Give yourself permission with soothing words like "it's alright, you can let me see this". Get used to the idea that you can 'turn once again to yourself' Luke 15:17 (or 'come to your senses'). Get used to the idea that you can talk to 'parts' (disciples) within you. Get used to the idea that your 'parts' (disciples) think very differently to you, and sometimes have vastly different beliefs to your core self.

Realise that you can develop a relationship with them. No matter how 'evil' (Matt7:11) they appear. No matter how much trouble they have got you in. No matter how demanding and forceful they seem. Like the disciples, they have been doing the best they can in the situation they are in. But what a relief when Jesus shows up and says, 'you can trust me'. Like the disciples, your brain is flexible, it is brilliant at rewiring itself. If you question this idea of flexibility, if you think that you can't do this, listen to Jesus' answer. "If I can? All things are possible to those that believe" (Mark 9:23).

So, make up your mind to meditate for a brief time each day. Think about a time in the last twenty-four hours where you have not behaved well or reacted out of proportion. Maybe it was your eating, drinking, or maybe your anger or fear. Look out for things you did that you said you would not do, or ways you said you would not be. Now spend a little time drawing up the mood, attitude, beliefs, feelings and behaviour as if it was someone else. Think about how old this person would have to be to feel or think that way. Now ask yourself which disciple this behaviour fits the most. Congratulations! You have started your inner discipling ministry.

Here is a short list of the questions I ask people to consider when getting to differentiate their parts from their self and from each other.

How old is my part?
Think about the first time you remember feeling this way

What does my part believe?
Think about the agenda this part has (what they need to happen)

What part is this part covering?
Think about what you were like before this part turned up

We don't have records of all the times the Lord corrected and taught the Disciples, but we have enough to understand and work with our various parts. We have enough to begin the work of discipling our parts and inspiring them to trust us. I will now use some examples to help you, but I would suggest doing your own study around this. Where you focus will depend on the type of struggles you have experienced.

Working in your 'upper room'

> Apart from me you can do nothing
>
> John 15:5

Remember earlier in the book where we learned about the upper room? When we internalise these ideas, we think of the upper room as the place where your parts become your disciples. It's where their earthly traits are transformed into a spiritually motivated life. It's where their strong emotions and agendas become the peace that passes all understanding. It's where the place of fear becomes the place of courage. If you are going to develop an authentic recovery, you will need to clean and purify your upper room. To win the hearts and minds of your disciples, you will first need to understand how the atmosphere changes when the Lord is present.

The TV screen of consciousness

All the inner work you do will be done through your consciousness. Consciousness is the secular word for the upper room. So, the first thing I want to say about this is that your consciousness is not you, any more than the upper room was the disciples. I want you to think of your consciousness like a TV screen in the room. A TV is something you own. It's yours to use. But sometimes we end up watching something we didn't mean to.

When you watch T.V. it should be up to you what you watch. You know that different programes will present different attitudes and appearances. The programes you watch will affect and influence you. We have all heard messages about what to avoid on the telly! Although you can't change what the different programs say and show, you can take more responsibility for which programes you watch. From now on, think of what goes on in your consciousness as a programe you are watching. Learning the difference between these channels will help you to ask, "Am I choosing to watch this programe"?

Separating your parts from your self

In the past you may have heard many messages encouraging you to be less like Thomas, Peter or less like Levi the tax collector. You may have heard a message telling you to be more like John. This is almost guaranteed to set up inner conflict since this teaching **mistakes the part for the self**. Don't mistake the disciple for the Lord!

It's only when you begin to see yourself as multifaceted that this separation (unblending) starts to make sense. As you read the following passage, please don't try to change anything. Yet!

Let's first look at the nature and characteristics of the disciples and the way these characteristics relate to our inner experience. Each of the disciples showed distinctive character traits as well as strengths and weaknesses. Jesus worked with them all. Developing them through His teaching and convicting them with the truth. In doing this, He showed us a way we can do this for ourselves. You may feel that you have already heard something that seems like this approach. Trust me, this is not the same. Let me explain.

Please be clear about this, it is here that the difference between a Biblical approach and the medical model is most clear. It is critical that you understand this difference. Jesus took responsibility for being the leader of the Disciples, but he always knew the difference! John 15 and verse 15 underlines this difference, and this relationship. The Bible is saying that these are 'parts' of you to be lovingly discipled. To make them friends. But never mistake them for yourself! (Romans 7:20) Whereas the medical approach defines them as simple examples of *'how you should not be'*, which always places you back **in conflict with yourself**.

As you become more aware of your parts presence through increased awareness of your upper room, as you learn more about your parts strategies and thoughts through developing the observer position. As you become more aware of the difference between Christ and the disciples, start to teach them, correct them and befriend them. This starts with letting them know who you are.

Neuroscience has shown us that your parts do not know who you really are. This might come as a shock to you, but it makes sense since they were all constructed at a certain age and know nothing beyond that time. Imagine meeting yourself as a youngster, you wouldn't think of questioning your younger self about what was happening years later. Think about how much more you know now, and how much more you have experienced. No younger self would be able to understand how much more you know than they do.

It was the same with the disciples. They did not really know who Jesus was at first. It was a process. Some got it faster than others. When you speak to your parts and begin to disciple them, do not have preconceived ideas about how long it will take for them to recognise who you are. Some will acknowledge you at once, like Peter. Others will take longer, like Thomas.

As you begin to develop better relationships with your 'parts', I want to encourage you to use a method I have found helpful. It includes these three ideas, **appreciation, education and negotiation**. Do whatever helps you to form better relationships, these three ideas are simply what I have developed to produce a coherent method.

Appreciation

Improving your relationship with your parts starts with appreciating some things about them. It starts with looking at what they are trying to do rather than what they are achieving. Always remember one thing, that they are trying their best to help you. They are giving you the best they have. They are never trying to screw up your life. Start with appreciating who they are. Jesus started this way. He said Follow me, and I will make you fishers of men. He appreciated what they were doing, but offered to show them who they really were!

Education

Educating your parts about **who you are** as part of the process is what comes next. Remember, trauma and difficulty in your life has trained them that they are on their own and must manage as best they can. You need to educate them that you are here, willing and able to manage this situation. Jesus said, "You call me 'Teacher' and 'Lord,' and rightly so, for that is what I am" (John 13:13). Tell them how much older than them you are, how much more experienced you are. Tell them what you know about their blessed assurance (John 15:15).

Negotiation

Once you have appreciated and educated, remember that they will only be drawn to you if they believe you. Do not slip back into old ways and try to force them. Never bully them or demand. Negotiate, ask them to consider allowing you to run things, especially around this thing that they are so concerned about. Tell them that no one who gives up things for the sake of the Kingdom of God will fail to receive many times as much, now and later (Luke18:29).

Remember to speak in an 'age appropriate' way. You can negotiate with an older part, but young children, toddlers and babies cannot be negotiated with. If you find that your parts will not listen to you or accept your leadership, just hold them! Let me take a minute to tell you about the time I learned about this.

One day in the store, I was in a long queue waiting to pay for my stuff. Ahead of me was a lady who was paying for her stuff. Under her arm was a toddler, he wasn't happy! He wanted a sweet and she was not giving him one. As far as he was concerned, this was the end of the world! I noticed that she was paying with one hand whilst holding him with the other.

As I was watching, my frustration melted away. I saw that a great lesson was unfolding before me. Here are a few things she was **not doing**.

1. She was not giving in to him
2. She was not allowing him to stop what she needed to do
3. She was not apologising to us for what he was doing
4. She was not trying to get him to 'change'

Some of your parts may be very young, they will not respond to negotiation. They need to be held and accepted, but not allowed to run your day! You need to accept that the feelings they bring, whilst being very strong, do not have to dictate your behaviour. Like this lady, you need to understand that these parts are too young to understand any of the complexities of life. But they will appreciate the security of being held. Of learning the boundaries of their power.

Sometimes you will be surprised at how quickly older parts will accept your authority. They do this because, like all youngsters, they would rather an adult turned up to deal with things. Remember, it's all about trust. Once they trust you to deal with a situation, they will trust you forever! Look at the disciple's level of trust when you read the book of Acts. That is what you will achieve once they know that you would die for them.

Different and Better

How do you know when you have made progress? How do we measure progress in this approach? I say to my clients "look for different and better". No matter how small the example, do not move on without spending time pulling your experience through this simple filter. Ask yourself "was this different (from how I have been reacting for years)? And was it better (as an outcome, from what I have been producing in the past)? If it was both, then move onto the next step, which is to **congratulate and celebrate**!

There are three forms of this, and they get progressively harder! The first form is thinking to yourself "I did well with that" or something like "I want more of that in my life". This is fine and helpful, but it is the weakest form of congratulating. The second form is saying it out loud! This is because the route into your brain is now through your ears, as well as in your mind. The third form is the strongest, if you can manage it! This is to stand in front of a mirror, eyeball yourself, and say it out loud. Now the information is in your mind, through your ears and through your eyes! Very powerful.

Jesus used this idea with Peter when he said "blessed are you, Simon, Son of Jonah. For this was not revealed to you by man, but by my Father in heaven." (Matt 16:17) Congratulating and celebrating spiritual progress. There are very good reasons to remark on these examples of progress, however small. It's because they are examples of evidence!

Brains change with evidence

Your brain, just like the disciples, transforms (rewires) through evidence. Your brain does not change because you changed your mind! Remember all those times when you said, "I will never do that again"? Didn't work, did it. All the motivational talks you have ever heard will not equal the power of one piece of evidence! Do not be discouraged. Congratulating and celebrating these moments is like doing exercise at the gym. Every bit of exercise is transforming you, no matter how small!

The disciple's transformational journey was based on evidence. When they were presented with a huge crowd to feed, their first reaction was to look to their own limitations. Yet they saw the glory of God when they trusted him, and five thousand people were fed. Mark 16:37-44

Now that you have the tools to practice with, I want to conclude with some more encouragement using Biblical examples and connecting them with your study and progress.

Know your disciples

> ONE DAY SOON AFTERWARD JESUS WENT UP ON A MOUNTAIN TO PRAY, AND HE PRAYED TO GOD ALL NIGHT. AT DAYBREAK HE CALLED TOGETHER ALL OF HIS DISCIPLES AND CHOSE TWELVE OF THEM TO BE APOSTLES. HERE ARE THEIR NAMES: SIMON (WHOM HE NAMED PETER), ANDREW (PETER'S BROTHER), JAMES, JOHN, PHILIP, BARTHOLOMEW, MATTHEW, THOMAS, JAMES (SON OF ALPHAEUS), SIMON (WHO WAS CALLED THE ZEALOT), JUDAS (SON OF JAMES), JUDAS ISCARIOT (WHO LATER BETRAYED HIM).
>
> LUKE 6:12/15

Studying the Bible and all the disciples will help you to get to know your own parts. Base your research on this principle; identify a triggered state as any time you are not in a state of calm, any time when you feel, think, speak or act out of proportion. By raising awareness of your different states, you will be more able to separate yourself from your parts. You can then begin to work with them from a place of compassion. Remember, the whole state, including body language, tone of voice, facial expression, thoughts, attitude, beliefs and behaviour *is* the part.

When you identify a triggered state, ask yourself, how old does that part seem to you? How is that part feeling, speaking and acting? At what age do people typically think, speak, or act like this? Once you get a sense of the age of your part, look around for old photos of yourself at that age. If you find one, place it on your bedside table. Now give this part a name and a description. It could be a nickname or a term of endearment your family or friends gave you. If the attitude reminds you of one of the disciples, then name them after him. This is mainly to separate your core self from your part. If, as a woman you don't feel comfortable giving your parts male names, stick to a descriptive name.

The description could be something basic and general, such as 'angry me' or 'sad me'. It may be 'the drinker', or 'the gambler'. The point is that you are getting to know who you will be working with by separating them from yourself. Here is a short list of things you will need to know concerning each part you want to disciple.

1. What is this parts name?
2. What is this parts age?
3. What does this part believe?
4. What does this part have me thinking, feeling and doing?

Jesus prayed all night to get to know who his disciples would be, and you need to meditate and pray likewise. Ask God in your prayers to show you the nature of your parts and how to disciple them. Once you have completed this you will have two things. A list of your inner disciples, and a picture of how they are relating to each other.

> Then his disciples began arguing about
> which of them was the greatest.
>
> Luke 9:46

You may not have realised this, but your parts do not always like each other. They will judge each other and think they are better than the others. This is known in theory as 'polarised parts'. They will often take opposing positions like when one part causes you to act out on your dependency or your weakness like anger or fear, a polarised part will judge you, and sometimes shame you or embarrass you. This will generally distract you by making you want to **try harder**. This will lead you into an eternal cycle of success and failure with no growth in sight. This is why it is so important to make sure that you are observing the part from your Christ minded state.

The parts will also be layered. This means that, as some are older than others, they will take the others' problems into account. One example of this is found in Matthew 26 verse 9 when some of them were indignant about the perfume used to anoint Jesus. Another example is the way Peter was accepted by the others as the leader of the group (John 21:3).

Let me give you a typical example from my practice to illustrate. I will often have a client who has a sad part that is around 5 years old, constructed when they were not given enough attention. To cope with this sadness, and the need to be heard, they developed an angry part around the age of 13, this part tries to help you by hiding or 'covering' the sad part. As a 16-year-old they then developed a drug taking part to cope with the constant anger outbursts. Etc. etc. Understanding this layering and the relationship between the parts is key to working with them more effectively.

Call your disciples

> "COME, FOLLOW ME," JESUS SAID, "AND I WILL SEND YOU OUT TO FISH FOR PEOPLE."
>
> MATTHEW 4:19

The next thing we need to do is to let the parts know that we are here, and who we are. It may seem strange to think that they do not know you. After all, they are part of you and live within you! But neuroscience has shown that they do not know anything beyond themselves. When working with a secular client, I ask them to think of their part as being of a certain age and therefore knowing nothing 'past' that age. For us as Christians, it is more useful to think of these parts as being spiritually immature. Consider the disciples when they first met Jesus. They knew that something incredibly special was happening, after all, some of them left everything and followed him! But they did not have anything like his spiritual maturity or wisdom.

Next, I want you to introduce yourself. Tell your parts who you are. How old you are and what experience you have. In the next section I will go into more detail about how to work with particular parts, and I will offer scriptural evidence of Jesus working with these traits in the Disciples. But for now, I want to offer you a general approach to introducing yourself and letting them know who you are to them. Jesus used all kinds of different approaches when discipling. Here are a few that we know of;

When Jesus saw Nathanael approaching, he said of him, "Here truly is an Israelite in whom there is no deceit." John 1:47. Here Jesus is using humour and maybe friendly sarcasm.

When the disciples James and John saw this, they asked, "Lord, do you want us to call fire down from heaven to destroy them?" But Jesus turned and rebuked them. Luke 9:54/55. Here Jesus is using direct correction.

This idea of knowing how to approach and work with your parts takes practice, but always remember two things. Firstly, that what we do will not always work straight away. We need to be patient and willing to develop a better relationship with these parts. Secondly, remember that the main thing we are doing with these parts is to help them to understand their authentic role in our lives. Jesus took fishermen, zealots and tax collectors and others, and helped them to understand their true destiny. Who they really were.

They thought they were fishermen,
but Christ showed them they were fishers of men.

In the fourth chapter of Matthew the Bible records that "As Jesus was walking beside the Sea of Galilee, he saw two brothers, Simon called Peter and his brother Andrew. They were casting a net into the lake, for they were fishermen. "Come, follow me," Jesus said, "and I will send you out to fish for people." At once they left their nets and followed him. Going on from there, he saw two other brothers, James's son of Zebedee and his brother John. They were in a boat with their father Zebedee, preparing their nets. Jesus called them, and at once they left the boat and their father and followed him". They thought they were fishermen, but Christ showed them they were fishers of men.

Your disciples will trust you too. Once they accept you as their Lord and master. Paul said to follow him as he follows Jesus (1 Cor 11:1). That is your message to your parts. You create a harmonised self as your parts learn to trust and obey you.

Love your disciples

> I NO LONGER CALL YOU SERVANTS, BECAUSE A SERVANT DOES NOT KNOW HIS MASTER'S BUSINESS. INSTEAD, I HAVE CALLED YOU FRIENDS, FOR EVERYTHING THAT I LEARNED FROM MY FATHER I HAVE MADE KNOWN TO YOU
>
> JOHN 15:15

When you first become aware of your parts you will realise that they have been there all along, but you have not thought of them as separate from you! You will also start to understand how some parts feel about other parts and why they have been covered, exiled or hated. You will understand more about why you have some parts that have been trained to be ashamed of other parts.

As you develop your awareness of your disciples, watch out for animosity or judgement. If you feel this when you think about a part, remember it's not you that is doing the thinking! This is simply one part judging another. There are many examples of this in the gospels (Luke 5:27). None of the other disciples would have respected Levi. He was a tax collector and would have been hated by every Jew. But Jesus' calling of Levi was the most public of all the disciples. He went to his house to eat a banquet prepared by Levi so all could see that Levi was welcome. Remember, your authentic Christ minded self will always view parts with compassion (Matt 9:36).

Just as the younger brother 'turned again to himself' (Luke 15:17) you can 'step back' to view these parts from your spirit. When you do, continue to look out for any animosity towards the part. Stop if this happens, as this always means that this is not your spirit but is simply one part judging another. The idea is to step back once more until you can view both parts, and the relationship between them. With practice, you will learn to 'step back' until you view these parts clearly from the right place. You will know when you have achieved this, because you will view all parts with compassion, or, put another way, through your Christ mindedness. Looking at your 'inner disciples' with pure compassion and connectedness is the only position that will bring about the progress needed. This is known as the 'observer position' and is the only position from which recovery can start.

In Mark 6 and verse 34 Jesus looked upon the crowd with compassion because they were like sheep without a Shepherd. Working with the Lord you will start to teach your parts many things. You will start to calm their fears, and, beyond that, your compassion for them will create harmony within you. A peace that passes all understanding (Phil 4:7)

Work with your Disciples

> ALL SCRIPTURE IS GOD-BREATHED AND IS USEFUL FOR TEACHING, REBUKING, CORRECTING AND TRAINING IN RIGHTEOUSNESS,
>
> 2 TIMOTHY 3:16

I know that this can be one of the most challenging ideas you might face. The idea of being in any way positive about your sinful nature. You have probably been taught to hate these things in yourself and you may have been taught to take the metaphor of the 'battle' too literally. So, if you are still struggling with this idea, go back to the chapter on 'from conflict to harmony', and take inspiration from the way that Jesus worked with the Disciples.

Loving your parts, who are just doing what they have been trained to do, only doing what they think is for the best, is where your harmonious life begins. After reassuring them that he loves them, Jesus says that he will **no longer** call them servants, but now will call them friends (John 15:15). This strongly implies a change of relationship, and this is the point. When you approach and think of your parts this way, they are no longer servants, just doing the best they know, from now on they will become friends. As you become the one who is closer than a brother (Proverbs 18:24) you are following Christ, and you are allowing Christ to work through you.

The change of relationship works both ways. Giving your inner disciples their proper job means accepting your role of Lord and Teacher to them. This can be difficult for many reasons. You may not think of yourself as a leader. You may not think of yourself as a teacher. 1 Corinthians Chapter two and verse 16 says For, 'Who has known the mind of the Lord so as to instruct him? But we have the mind of Christ'. It may seem difficult to you to accept that when you are in your 'core state' you and Jesus are **one thing**. But this is how God works! Think about the Gospels, who wrote them? Was it Matthew Mark Luke and John? Or was it God? Of course, it was both together. Similarly, when you are doing Gods will you and Christ are one through the Holy Spirit.

One of the best examples of this is Matthew 16, in verse 17 Jesus blesses Simon because in speaking words 'from God' he becomes inseparable from God. This leads to the name change and Simon becomes Peter. Jesus also confirms that from this position nothing can overcome us. The 'rock' that the Church will be built upon is not Peter, but the aligning of ourselves with God.

Another example is in 1 Corinthians Chapter 6 and verse 17 where Paul confirms that "whoever is united with the Lord is one with him in spirit." It may be difficult for you to grasp and believe this Biblical truth, so take your time and make sure you have understood the implications of this idea.

The more you practice this, the more you will understand your core state, the more you will allow yourself to speak authoritatively from this position, and the more you will win the trust of your inner disciples. I now want to talk specifically about what Jesus taught us about working with various parts.

Angry parts

> WHEN THE DISCIPLES SAW THIS, THEY WERE INDIGNANT. "WHY THIS WASTE?" THEY ASKED.
>
> MATTHEW 26:8

The NIV says indignant, other versions say angry! But notice how Jesus manages this anger. He points out that their concern is very worldly and that there are higher things being done. In verse 11 he says that the poor you will always have with you, but you will not always have me. This is to remind them that these earthly issues will always be around, but that their attention should be on the higher things. This is another way of saying 'trust me' in your attitudes and thinking.

We see this again in Matthew 16 and verse 23 when he rebukes Peter saying that he has in mind the things of man, not the things of God. Your parts behave the way they do for the same reason the Disciples do, because the world has trained them to be that way. The Disciples' attitudes and behaviour was shaped by the world they lived in, and it's the same for your parts. The Disciples wanted to look after the Lord the best way they knew how, but Jesus taught them to trust Him. He did not need or want to be protected from these things, because it was His Fathers will that He endure them. It's your job to teach your parts that they do not need to protect you from these things either.

Always remember when working with angry parts of you, or any other type of part that embarrasses or shames you, that they are always doing what they think is best. They are doing what the world has taught them to do. They are doing what they know. Don't be thinking that you shouldn't be firm with them. Remember that you are the boss and should talk from this position. Just remember to do it the way Jesus did, educating and building them up at the same time.

Shamed parts

> Then Jesus said to her, "Your sins are forgiven."
> Luke 7:48

Shame is a crucial factor in our lives because it is sinful in and of itself, but worse, it encourages us to cover up the sin it connects with. Your shamed parts are protecting you by pressuring you to not reveal your other parts. If no one sees it, then it's like it never happened! This becomes a habit and creates what is now known as a neural pathway, which is a form of 'mental cliche'.

Like a cart following the grooves made in the ground through continual use, your brain will continue to follow this 'train of thought' until you change it. Always remember that everything you do and everything you say trains your brain into that pattern. The Disciples had been trained by hundreds of years of religious practice, by their families, and by their culture.

When Jesus is challenged by the religious leader that he is being touched by a sinful woman (Luke 7:39), he connects him with shame as a way of shaming Him. This is a common strategy of religious control, which comes from the idea that we are corrupted by the sin we connect with in others. Jesus responds with his own challenge. He offers a parable and asks the man who loves God more, he who has been forgiven more, or he who has been forgiven less. The one who has been forgiven more, responds the man. Jesus exposes the religious fraud by appreciating what the woman brought (her great love) and comparing it with the lack of love which results from religious snobbery.

If you have a shaming part, take time to remind the part that you are here, and that you are willing and able to manage the other parts and so there is no need to protect you from them any longer. Make sure that your part understands that you appreciate that they did the best they knew and that they tried hard to manage things. That they are forgiven for any past behaviour and that they are welcome. Pay particular attention to the idea that you are happy to be connected with them.

Anxious parts

> SUDDENLY A FURIOUS STORM CAME UP ON THE LAKE, SO THAT THE WAVES SWEPT OVER THE BOAT. BUT JESUS WAS SLEEPING. THE DISCIPLES WENT AND WOKE HIM, SAYING, "LORD, SAVE US! WE'RE GOING TO DROWN!"
>
> MATTHEW 8:24/25

You may not have a history of acting with strength and authority. Certain things in life may have been triggering you into allowing a panicky part to dictate your behaviour and feelings, to take over your thoughts and even your actions. When Jesus sees this panic in the Disciples, He reminds them that they are acting with 'little faith'. He asks them why are you afraid? This is all part of his teaching and training them to trust Him completely. To not act out of panic but to trust Him with the answer and the direction they will take.

As you practice this with your own Disciples, you might see what Jesus saw, that they do not believe straight away! There are many examples of this lack of belief in the Gospels. Do not stop the practice, continue to talk to them. Continue to assure them that you are willing and able to handle this situation, if they will trust you with it. Remember to approach these situations with the authority that Jesus did. You have the mind of Christ!

Unbelieving parts

> SO THE OTHER DISCIPLES TOLD HIM, "WE HAVE SEEN THE LORD!" BUT HE SAID TO THEM, "UNLESS I SEE THE NAIL MARKS IN HIS HANDS AND PUT MY FINGER WHERE THE NAILS WERE, AND PUT MY HAND INTO HIS SIDE, I WILL NOT BELIEVE."
>
> JOHN 20:25

When we see doubting parts we are reminded of Thomas. It seems that no amount of words or reasoning will do for these parts. They want proof! What did Jesus do? In verse 26 he said to Thomas, "Put your finger here; see my hands. Reach out your hand and put it into my side. Stop doubting and believe."

I want you to approach your doubting parts the same way. If there are still doubts no matter how you talk to them, then offer them the same deal that Jesus offered Thomas. Say to them "I know you are struggling to believe that I can handle this situation but let me make a deal with you. Let me handle this now and see how I do. See for yourself how I manage this. If I don't manage it well. You can always come back and take over the next time.

We must be bold and confident. This will always be true when we are in our Christ mindedness.

Egotistical parts

> "WHAT IS IT YOU WANT?" HE ASKED. SHE SAID, "GRANT THAT ONE OF THESE TWO SONS OF MINE MAY SIT AT YOUR RIGHT AND THE OTHER AT YOUR LEFT IN YOUR KINGDOM."
>
> MATTHEW 20:21

Most of us have some egotistical parts. The first problem can be accepting that they exist! It can be embarrassing to think of yourself this way. Remind yourself of Jeremiah 6:14 and don't try to heal something by pretending it's not there. Accept that you have an egotistical part and make up your mind to disciple it! Let's look at how Jesus handled this in his disciples.

When this outrageous request came to Jesus from the mother of James and John, Jesus asked them if they could do what He was about to do, if they could go through what He was about to go through. Ego was present again when they said, "we can". And this offers us a great insight to working with ego in our disciples. You cannot approach blindness by asking it to see something! They could not understand what they were asking or what Jesus was asking them in return! Be patient with these parts. Allow experience to alter their attitude about intervening in your day.

When the other disciples heard about this request, they became indignant with the two who had asked. This was more ego and a desire to be first in line. You may have experienced this in your life and as the Lord convicted you, you may have become ashamed and tried to hide it. But look at how the Lord handles this situation. He reminds them that in His Kingdom those who want to be first, achieve this by being last. They become the greatest by being the least of all. Their aim should be to serve all others.

Another example of the egotistical part comes from the book of Philippians. In the fourth Chapter we hear Paul plead with Euodia and Syntyche to be "of the same mind in the Lord". Since the whole of Philippians is about being spiritually stable, we can safely assume what he is talking about here. He is not saying that they are in error as far as the word of God is concerned. If that was the case, then he would have simply corrected one or the other of them. He is asking them to be in harmony with each other, by being in harmony with themselves.

We are all prone to favouring certain relationships over others, and some people always seem to 'rub us up the wrong way'. Here is a case in point. Some friction had grown between these two women and Paul is asking them to get into the right mindset, which is Christs mindset (1 Cor 2:16). Notice how Paul contrasts their state with the person he is speaking to directly. In verse 3 he says "yes, and I ask you, true companion". The Greek word here is translated as 'yokefellow'. This could mean someone with this name, or the whole Church. Of course, 'true' can also mean authentic. So, Paul is asking the people who are truly 'Christ minded' to help these women. In the same way, your authentic Christ minded self can help the part of you that is caught up in ego disputes.

Ask your egotistical part to trust Christ in you. Ask particularly that this part should trust the idea that you must suffer in some ways and that your victory will come, not by being first in line, but by being last and least. Remember that when you work with these parts, they may not change their egotistical attitudes. The important thing is that they will trust you to handle things and not intervene.

Grandiose parts

> Peter took him aside and began to rebuke him. "Never, Lord!" he said. "This shall never happen to you!"
>
> Matthew 16:22

When trying to understand any part of you that tries to protect you with grandiose claims, think about Peter in the situation above. In Matthew 16:22 Peter is being grandiose because he is making claims that he cannot live up to. He does this in several diverse ways recorded in the Gospels. Jesus has been teaching them this, admittedly difficult idea, that he is about to be crucified and will rise on the third day. This is exceedingly difficult for them to hear because they have been taught for countless generations that the Messiah will come and free them by force. So, it is understandable that they would react to such an idea. But Peter is taking Jesus aside and rebuking him!

Coming to terms with our abilities and our limitations is such an important part of our progress, but your grandiose part will try to protect you by introducing outlandish claims about your own abilities, and what you will be able to do.

Remember that grandiosity is thinking you are special and the most important person. Jesus aims his teaching at the whole group when he corrects Peter. In verse 24 he says 'Then Jesus said to his disciples, "Whoever wants to be my disciple must deny themselves and take up their cross and follow me. For whoever wants to save their life will lose it, but whoever loses their life for me will find it.

Frightened parts

> "YOU AREN'T ONE OF THIS MAN'S DISCIPLES TOO, ARE YOU?"
> SHE ASKED PETER. HE REPLIED, "I AM NOT."
>
> JOHN 18:17

The more immediate the danger and threat, the quicker and the stronger the brain/flesh reaction. Remember that you cannot stop this reaction! Remind yourself whenever this happens that you could not stop this from happening. This is always the first step because keeping a good relationship with yourself is necessary to bring about progress and the type of development you are needing.

If you have a frightened part that reacts like this, then you understand some of what Peter went through when he wept bitter tears of regret (Matthew 26:75). When we are faced with our human weakness in such a stark and brutal way, we are often drawn into a conflicted position, hating ourselves because we feel that we should be doing better, or that we should have learned by now! These feelings are intensified when we do not continue to make a strong distinction between the parts and yourself. Make sure that you have made the transforming move from medical to Biblical thinking (Romans 12:2).

Notice Jesus' response to Peter's weakness. Remember that he already knew what would happen (Matthew 26:34). Although Peter was discouraged to the point of forgetting the job Jesus had given him. Even though he had returned to fishing, the next time Jesus saw him there was no judgement, there was no rebuke. There was no criticism, no shaming comments. Jesus went to the shore where he knew Peter would be and cooked him breakfast! Jesus asks Peter to confirm his love and reminds him of the job He gave him. To feed his lambs.

When reactions are so intense and so quick it is even more important to check that you are working from the observer position. Continually checking your compassion for your lost sheep. It is only from this position that your Christ mindedness can bring perfect peace, confidence and compassion to your situation. Once you are 'observing' from the correct position you can remind your part that they have a job to do for you, and you can remind the part of how much you value them in your life.

What will overcoming look like?

With practice and perseverance, your parts will learn to trust you as the disciples learned to trust Christ. The evidence for this will depend on the struggles you have had in your life. Whatever the nature of the problems the outcome will be the same. You will notice that you (authentic Christ minded you) are increasingly allowed to run your own life. Beliefs you hold about what good behaviour and thinking looks like will be more manifest in your daily living. You will be able to make decisions and stick to them! What once appeared impossible for you will become easy and effortless. I see this type of transformation in people I work with every day.

One thing to watch out for as you make progress is trying too hard! This is very common and denotes a slipping back into the medical model. Nowhere in this book have you been told to try hard. Forcing your brain to comply against its best wishes for your safety will inevitably draw you back into conflict with yourself. If this happens, forgive yourself and take some time to meditate and learn from your experiences. Read Jesus prayer for us in John Chapter seventeen, reminding yourself that his pray for you and me is inner harmony. When your brain trusts you, you will be free to run your own life without fighting or forcing, pretending or hiding.

Does this mean that you will never be in a triggered state again? No, you will never be perfect this side of heaven. Paul writes very clearly about this when he says that this glory is kept in jars of clay (2 Cor 4:7). So that we never forget that this all-surpassing power comes from God and not from us.

Conclusion

In this book you have been challenged to shift the way you think about yourself from a medical to a Biblical view. In conclusion, I want to make sure that you have not missed any of the vital steps in this journey. Here is a list of what I would want you to have understood and added to your practice by reading this book.

1. The difference between the medical model and the Biblical model (Chapter One)
2. That your multifaceted nature is normal and designed (Chapter Two)
3. How much the medical model has influenced you (Chapter Three)
4. A better understanding of your sinful nature (Chapter Three)
5. That your issues are solutions that became problems (Chapter Three)
6. That forcing yourself to change is often counterproductive (Chapter Three)
7. That your relationship with yourself is the best place to start (Chapter Three)
8. That God has left us a working method to follow (Chapter Four)
9. That you can use the way Jesus discipled to work with your inner self (Chapter Five)
10. That your brain has been trained to take over when threatened (Chapter Six)
11. That your flesh (parts/disciples) is always trying to help you (Chapter Seven)

12. That you can create inner harmony working with these parts of you (Chapter Eleven)
13. That your 'parts' will learn to trust you once you produce evidence (Chapter Twelve)
14. That this will be sometimes a quick process and sometimes a slow one (Chapter Twelve)

I have spent the past forty years developing my own recovery and spiritual growth, as well as working with people who have suffered with addiction and reverse addiction. I wish had known what I now know when I first started. The results I am getting now are far better since I stopped thinking of people as sick, broken, and faulty and started thinking of them as Gods masterpiece! I hope this book has inspired you to look at yourself from this perspective. I want to encourage you to ask yourself "what if everything that's happening to me is because of how well I am working, not because of how faulty I am?" This question changed everything in my life, and it can do the same for you.

Further resources
https://buildingrecovery.org/

www.ingramcontent.com/pod-product-compliance
Lightning Source LLC
Chambersburg PA
CBHW052138070526
44585CB00017B/1880